WITHDRAWN

3o~minute jewellery

60 quick and easy jewellery projects

beverly mccullough

Search Press

This edition published in 2015 by

Search Press Ltd

Wellwood

North Farm Road

Tunbridge Wells

Kent, TN2 3DR, UK

www.searchpress.com

A Quintet book

Copyright © 2015 Quintet Publishing Limited

QTT.TMJ

All rights reserved. No part of this publication may be
reproduced or distributed in any form or by any means
without the written permission of the copyright owner.

ISBN: 978-1-78221-277-5

This book was designed and produced by

Quintet Publishing Limited

4th Floor, Sheridan House,

114-116 Western Road,

Hove, BN3 1DD, UK

Project Editor: Caroline Elliker
Designer: Tania Gomes
Step Illustrator: Mark Watkinson
Photographer: Sussie Bell
Art Director: Michael Charles
Editorial Director: Alana Smythe
Publisher: Mark Searle

Printed in China by 1010 Printing Group Limited

9 8 7 6 5 4 3 2 1

contents

introduction

Jewellery making doesn't have to be intimidating or difficult. It's so easy to create beautiful pieces that are perfect for your style and wardrobe in just a few minutes. Whether you are starting out on your jewellery-making adventure, or you've been making fun accessories for years, this book has all sorts of projects that will inspire and excite you to start creating!

My personal style leans towards vintage with a little bit of quirkiness – and you'll definitely find pieces in this book representing that style. The fabulous thing about creating your own jewellery is that it is simple to take a specific technique and change it to fit your taste, just by substituting beads or materials. The pieces in *30-Minute Jewellery* are a fun mix of modern, classic, playful and glamorous designs.

This book begins with basic projects which are perfect for learning new skills if you are just starting out or extra quick to create for more experienced jewellery makers. As you develop your skills, you'll easily progress through the intermediate and advanced projects in no time at all.

There is a fun mix of methods as well – you will find everything from basic wire work to embroidery and sewing. One of my favourite aspects of jewellery making is upcycling unique materials and creating pieces that are original and stylish at the same time. I've provided resource websites at the back of the book where I found some of my more unique supplies, but if you are unable to find specific items listed, or would prefer a different overall colour or style, feel free to substitute them for similar items according to your preferences. Also, if you are a beginner, don't be discouraged if some of the more advanced pieces take longer than thirty minutes to make. As you become more proficient with these new skills, you will find the projects easier and quicker to create.

My hope is that *30-Minute Jewellery* will start you on the road to a love for jewellery making that will lead you to develop your own skills and style. As you gain more confidence, you'll soon be creating new designs and pieces to accentuate your wardrobe or to give as gifts. Enjoy!

30~minute projects

basic

faceted bead necklace *page 11*

jewelled cuff *page 12*

dip dyed earrings *page 15*

pastel drop earrings *page 16*

polka dot and button cuff *page 18*

clay diamond earrings *page 19*

dipped crystal pendant *page 20*

home sweet home necklace *page 23*

sweet as honey bangle *page 24*

woodland scene ring *page 27*

fabric bead earrings *page 28*

thread wrapped bangles *page 31*

mini masterpiece necklace *page 32*

micro bead ring *page 34*

porcelain piece necklace *page 35*

rings and beads bracelet *page 36*

map bangle *page 39*

fabric and leather watch *page 40*

rhinestone wrapped earrings *page 43*

time for tea ring *page 44*

intermediate

daisy earrings *page 47*

braided leather bracelet *page 48*

wire wrapped geode necklace *page 49*

feather and chain earrings *page 50*

charm stretch bracelet *page 52*

vintage ribbon and beads necklace *page 53*

lace drop earrings *page 55*

peaches and cream necklace *page 56*

embroidered monogram ring *page 59*

pearl drop earrings *page 60*

bright chain cuff
page 63

leather chevron
necklace *page 64*

thread wrapped
earrings *page 67*

clay bow necklace
page 68

acrylic dangle earrings
page 71

cat's meow necklace
page 72

cord and clasp
bracelets *page 73*

pearl stacking
rings *page 75*

tassel chain earrings
page 76

beaded strand
bracelet *page 79*

advanced

lace and pearl
pendant *page 81*

colourful bar
bracelet *page 82*

ombré crystal
earrings *page 83*

beaded chandelier
earrings *page 85*

wrapped bead rings
page 86

silver lining necklace
page 89

fabric and rings
bracelets *page 90*

embroidered rose
brooch *page 93*

wooden scallops
necklace *page 94*

floating beads
necklace *page 96*

cluster pendant
page 97

bead and chain
bracelet *page 99*

crystallised hoop
earrings *page 100*

bars and beads
necklace *page 103*

felt hedgehog brooch
page 104

necktie cuff
page 107

embroidered fox
necklace *page 108*

beaded drop earrings
page 111

braided chain
necklace *page 112*

multi-chain
bracelet *page 114*

faceted bead necklace

This faceted bead necklace is so stylish yet so simple to make. There are endless options for creating with these fun beads, too: you could paint them entirely, mix and match the colours, or leave them as natural wood and just accent a bead or two on the necklace.

MATERIALS

7 × 20mm faceted wooden beads

8 × 6mm beads

102cm (40in) length of 1mm leather cording

Wood stain

White paint pen

Orange paint pen

INSTRUCTIONS

1. Apply wood stain to the faceted beads, following the manufacturer's instructions.

2. Once the stain is completely dry, select a few sides of each bead and fill in with the white paint pen. Use the white paint pen to also outline the edges of the facets on all the beads. You might need two or three coats of paint for complete coverage and a nice, bright look.

3. On the sides of the beads that have been painted white, outline the edges with the orange paint pen. Again, you may need to apply a few coats so the paint is nice and bright.

4. Once all the paint is dry, lay out the leather cording. Begin by stringing on a small 6mm bead, then add a faceted wooden bead. Alternate the small beads and wooden beads, ending with a small bead.

5. Finish the cording with two adjustable sliding knots. Trim the ends of the cording to 12mm (½in) past each knot. Adjust the necklace to the desired length, but don't lengthen it so much that the knots are touching.

projects

jewelled cuff

It takes just a few minutes to make this designer-style, sparkly jewelled cuff at a fraction of the cost of shop-bought jewellery. You can create almost any pattern and choose how much, or how little, of the cuff you would like to decorate. Try wrapping the metal cuff in fabric first for a colourful variation.

INSTRUCTIONS

1. Choose a lace fabric design with pretty shapes within the lace, making it easier to cut out. Do not leave loose threads. Cut out the section of your choice for the base of the jewelled decoration. The pictured panel measures 4 × 4cm (1½ × 1½in).

2. Lay the rhinestones on the lace panel, arranging them as desired. Try mixing a variety of different shapes and colours to make the overall design more interesting.

3. Cut a few rhinestones from the rhinestone strand and add to the lace panel, filling any open areas in the jewelled design.

4. Glue the jewels in place on the lace and leave to dry. Once these are set, glue the lace panel in place on the centre front of the cuff.

TIP

If you are struggling to find rhinestones in colours you like, purchase clear ones and paint them with a light coat of nail polish followed by a coat of glossy sealer. It's easy to create your own custom coloured rhinestones in just a few minutes!

MATERIALS

Wide metal cuff bracelet

Lace motif in your choice of shape (see instructions for details)

Assorted rhinestone jewels in settings

Rhinestone strand trim

Jewellery glue

EQUIPMENT

Wire cutters

Scissors

dip dyed earrings

Plastic dyeable beads were a recent find for me. They are such fun to dye and you can create so many different looks. I'm in love with this pink tinted pair, but I've also made a deep turquoise version. They are quick to create as well; the length of making time depends on how dark you want the dye on the beads to be.

MATERIALS

2 × matt plastic beads (best if labelled 'dyeable')

2 × head pins

2 × kidney ear wires

Satin decoupage

Liquid dye

Disposable bowl

EQUIPMENT

Small paintbrush

Wire cutters

Round nose pliers

Flat nose pliers

INSTRUCTIONS

1. Add a plastic bead to each head pin and make a loop at the top.

2. Place the liquid dye in a disposable bowl. Add a small amount of water to dilute – the more water you add, the lighter the dye on the beads will be.

3. Place the beads in the dye and leave them until they are as saturated in colour as you would like.

4. To give the beads an ombré effect, place a wire through the head pin loops at the top of the beads and rest the wire across the top of the bowl. Start with the beads completely submerged, then bend the wire to slowly raise them out of the dye, leaving the bottom portion of the beads in the dye the longest.

5. Set your beads out to dry. Hang them up if possible, so the dye doesn't settle on the beads.

6. Once the dye is dry, brush the beads with a light coat of satin decoupage to set the dye and protect it from fading or rubbing off.

7. Secure the head pin loops to the ear wires to finish.

pastel drop earrings

Elegant drop earrings are so easy and fun to make. Beads already in settings are becoming more readily available, especially online, and they come in a huge variety of pretty colours and styles. If you can't find the pre-set beads to suit your look, settings and beads are available separately in a large number of shops – it takes just a few extra minutes to create your own custom set beads.

MATERIALS

2 × oval beads in settings with a loop at each end

2 × round beads

2 × head pins

2 × ear wires

EQUIPMENT

Wire cutters

Round nose pliers

Flat nose pliers

INSTRUCTIONS

1. Place one of the round beads on a head pin and make a loop at the top.

2. Open the loop and secure it to the bottom loop of the oval bead setting.

3. Open the ear wire loop and secure it to the top loop of the oval bead setting.

4. Repeat for the second earring.

TIP

When using beads and head pins to make earrings, it is especially important to create equally sized loops. Having one loop larger than the other will make the earrings hang at different lengths. If you find that the loops are of varying sizes, it is much easier to cut the pin off and recreate the loop, rather than trying to correct it. Adjusting the loop too much will weaken it, making it more likely to break.

polka dot and button cuff

Mix and match different fabrics, buttons and embellishments to customise and change the look of this shabby chic style cuff. A pretty floral fabric paired with black and white buttons; a fun, bright pattern coupled with pastels; or even a lace cuff with antique gold buttons. The options are endless.

MATERIALS

Metal cuff bracelet

2.5cm (1in) wide, 112cm (44in) length of fabric

Assortment of buttons

Rhinestone strand

Jewellery glue

EQUIPMENT

Wire cutters

Scissors

INSTRUCTIONS

1. Leaving a 2.5cm (1in) overhang of fabric, fold the fabric strip around one end of the cuff and glue it in place.

2. Tuck the overhang of the strip to the inside of the cuff and wrap the long end around it, gluing it in place.

3. Continue wrapping the fabric around the cuff, occasionally adding a small amount of glue to secure it on the inside of the cuff. Once the entire cuff is wrapped, fold the strip around the end and glue in place. Finally, wrap the fabric over the end and fold to the inside.

4. Trim the ends and glue in place on the inside of the cuff.

5. Layer an assortment of buttons in place over the centre of the cuff. Buttons with shanks work best here, as they generally have decorative tops, but you can use any type. Cut the shanks off the buttons with the wire cutter, if necessary, so they lay flat. Glue in place.

6. To finish off the cuff, wrap a small strip of rhinestone strand around a few of the buttons, and glue it in place to add sparkle.

TIP

Achieve a few different looks by altering the way in which you wrap the fabric around the cuff. For a more rustic, casual look, tear the fabric and leave the ends on to show fray. Alternatively, fold the edges in as you wrap for a cleaner look. You could even experiment with different fabrics, such as lace, or layer different trims for a multicoloured base and modern look.

clay diamond earrings

Who needs expensive diamond earrings when you can create your own colourful versions for a fraction of the cost? With a small amount of clay, you can have a whole rainbow of earrings in just a few minutes.

MATERIALS

2 × brass diamond shapes – sample measures 15 15 2mm

2 × contrasting shades of one colour of polymer clay

Flat earring posts and backs

Jewellery glue

Parchment paper

EQUIPMENT

Oven

INSTRUCTIONS

1. Lay out a piece of parchment paper to protect the work surface and to keep the clay clean. Tear off two small pieces from each of the polymer clay colours. Separately work each piece of clay in your hands until it is soft and pliable.

2. Fold the two pieces of clay together and continue blending them until the colours form a marble pattern. Be careful not to overwork the clay or you will lose the marble effect and the colours will blend together completely.

3. Roll a small amount of the clay into a ball and press it into one of the brass diamond shapes. Keep pressing until the clay fills the entire shape and you have formed a slightly curved indention. Smooth out the clay to remove any fingerprints. Repeat for the second diamond shape.

4. Place a piece of parchment paper on a baking sheet and position your earrings onto the parchment paper. Bake the clay according to the directions on the packaging.

5. Once the clay is cooled, check to see if it is loose in its setting. If so, pop it out, add a thin layer of jewellery glue to the inside of the diamond shape and replace the clay. Glue the earring posts to the back of the clay.

TIP

Clay will pick up all sorts of dust and fibres, so make sure you are working on a clean surface and wash your hands regularly.

dipped crystal pendant

This crystal necklace is the perfect statement piece to dress up a monochrome outfit or to layer with one or two other simple necklaces. There are so many colours of crystals available that you could create a few for a whole rainbow of accessories. Try adding a small charm or a few beads on a jump ring at the top of the pendant for a different, but equally pretty finish.

MATERIALS

Crystal piece – crystal shown measures 12 35mm

Gold paint pen

Masking tape

Gold glue-on bail

61cm (24in) necklace chain

Lobster clasp

9mm jump ring

2 × 5mm jump rings

Jewellery glue

EQUIPMENT

Needle nose pliers

Flat nose pliers

TIP

Washi tape, a decorative tape, can be used in place of masking tape. It is similar to masking tape in that it is easy to apply and remove and it does a great job of keeping the paint in place, with the added bonus of looking cute at the same time.

INSTRUCTIONS

1. Tape off the lower section of the crystal at an angle. Press the tape tightly all around the crystal to try to stop the paint from seeping through.

2. Paint the entire lower section of the crystal, applying two coats if necessary to get a neat, even coverage. Leave to dry thoroughly.

3. Once the paint is dry, remove the tape. If any paint has seeped under, it can be removed with a pin or a craft knife.

4. Glue the bail to the back of the crystal at the top. Choose the section that is the highest point of the crystal for the back, so it will sit nicely when worn.

5. Once the bail is dry, feed the chain through the loop and create your necklace closure using the lobster clasp and jump rings.

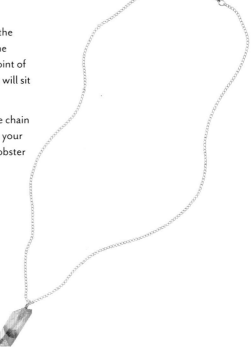

home sweet home necklace

One of my favourite things about this necklace is the little house charm, but the necklace style makes it perfect for any charm you find. It would be so cute with a tiny ballet slipper, or maybe a football, or how about a spool of thread? It is easy to customise for most hobbies or personal styles, making it ideal for gifts, too.

MATERIALS

Metal filigree piece with a centre large enough for the charm

Spray paint in your choice of colour (shown in coral)

House charm, or other decorative charm

Small scrap of fabric for bow

46cm (18in) length of jewellery chain

4 × 6mm jump rings

Lobster clasp

Jewellery glue

EQUIPMENT

Needle nose pliers

Flat nose pliers

Scissors

INSTRUCTIONS

1. Spray paint the metal filigree piece in your chosen colour and leave it to dry thoroughly. If you prefer, you can leave the filigree unpainted, but the colour provides a pretty contrast to the charm.

2. Once the paint is dry, add the charm to a jump ring, then add the jump ring to the central section of the filigree piece.

3. Add a jump ring to the top of the filigree piece — do this before attaching the bow to prevent the bow from fraying.

4. Form the fabric into a small bow and trim off any loose fabric threads. Glue the bow in place at the top of the filigree piece. Make sure to keep the top jump ring free of glue.

5. Once everything is dry, feed the chain through the top jump ring and finish the necklace with the jump rings and lobster clasp.

TIP

When gluing objects with open details, such as this filigree piece, place the items on a piece of parchment paper before gluing them together. The glue won't stick to the paper and you will have an easy clean up.

sweet as honey bangle

For the longest time I was against gold jewellery, and pretty much stuck to silver in my designs, but now I've completely fallen in love with the look of gold. I especially like it when used with other colours, as I think it really sets them off and makes them stand out. That's just the case with this bangle. It's lovely as a plain mint green bracelet, but the gold accentuates the edges and takes the whole piece to the next level.

MATERIALS

Wooden honeycomb bangle

Mint green acrylic paint (use spray paint if preferred)

Medium edge gold paint pen

Glossy spray finish

EQUIPMENT

Paintbrush

INSTRUCTIONS

1. Paint the bangle in your chosen colour. I recommend starting with the outside and one edge, allowing it to dry before moving to the opposite edge and then finally painting the inside. This system helps to prevent drips from forming in the paint and gives you a place to hold the bangle as you work.

2. Once the paint is completely dry, outline the raised edges of the honeycombs with the gold paint pen and cover the top edge of the bangle at the same time. Once this edge is completely dry, paint the other edge of the bangle and go over any honeycomb edges that need more coverage.

3. To give the bangle a sleek shine, spray it with a glossy finish sealer. If you prefer a matt finish, I still recommend using some sort of sealant, maybe a satin decoupage, to prevent the paint from scratching off when bumped.

TIP

This bangle would look fabulous in so many colours! Think soft pastels for a pretty spring version, earth tones for an autumn-inspired version, or even white or black for a striking contrast with the gold.

woodland scene ring

This whimsical woodland ring is so unique and fun – it's the perfect way to take a little of the outdoors with you wherever you go. You can easily create any scene your heart desires. Choose from the many different kinds of resin items available through online suppliers or create your own shapes from polymer clay.

MATERIALS

7mm resin mushroom

Small amount of moss

9 × 15mm glass dome

15mm setting based ring blank

Toothpick

Jewellery glue

INSTRUCTIONS

1. Cut a small piece of the moss. Spread a thin layer of jewellery glue into the blank of the ring and place the moss in the glue. Try to keep the moss central, covering all the way to the edges of the blank.

2. Place a good amount of glue on the bottom of the resin mushroom and place it in the centre of the moss on the ring blank. Hold in place for a little while to set the glue, so the mushroom stays put when you position the dome.

3. Once the mushroom is securely set in place, spread a ring of glue around the edge of the blank. Use a toothpick to enable you to also move the moss out of the way as you work. Glue the dome over the mushroom and press onto the ring blank, making sure you don't have any moss outside of the dome. Hold in place until well set.

TIP

You don't want the resin centrepiece to tip over inside the dome while everything is drying, so ideally dry the ring sitting vertically. Create a simple, inexpensive drying rack by cutting a slit into a small square of Styrofoam with a knife. Insert the circular portion of the ring into the slit and leave it securely in place to dry.

fabric bead earrings

Fabric covered beads look tricky to make, but they are really quite simple and there is no sewing involved. These earrings are so cute with their colourful floral beads, but wouldn't they also be fun with a black-and-white geometric print?

INSTRUCTIONS

1. Wrap a fabric strip around the first bead. Trim the fabric so it just overlaps around the widest part of the bead. Press the fabric up to the top of the bead with your finger – the top and bottom should overlap the hole by about 6mm (¼in). Trim off any extra fabric.

2. Hold the bead so the hole runs vertically through it. Brush the decoupage around the middle of the bead. Wrap the fabric around the bead and overlap it. Hold until the fabric stays in place.

3. Cut vertical strips in the top of the fabric, down to where the fabric is attached to the bead, cutting the fabric every 3mm (⅛in) or so.

4. Brush the decoupage over the top of the bead. Begin pressing the strips down on the top of the bead. Feed the end into the hole and press in place with the skewer. Continue overlapping the strips to cover the top of the bead, adding more decoupage as necessary. Repeat for the bottom of the bead.

5. Add a 4mm bead to a head pin, then the fabric-covered bead, then another 4mm bead. Form a loop at the top. Add the loop to the loop at the bottom of an ear wire.

6. Repeat for the second earring.

MATERIALS

2 × 20mm round wooden beads with large opening

2 × pieces of fabric – 5 × 7.5cm (2 3in)

Decoupage

4 × 4mm beads

2 × head pins

2 × ear wires

EQUIPMENT

Round nose pliers

Flat nose pliers

Wire cutters

Paintbrush

Scissors

Pencil or a skewer – something that will fit in the hole of the bead

thread wrapped bangles

These bangles are so cute and easy to make. Each one takes just a little while to wrap, and you can have a lot of fun mixing up the colour schemes. They look so pretty stacked up in multiples, too.

MATERIALS

Wooden bangle

2 colours of crewel embroidery thread

White paint

Glossy spray sealant

EQUIPMENT

Paintbrush

Embroidery needle

INSTRUCTIONS

1. Paint the bangle white – you might need to apply a few coats to ensure complete coverage.

2. Once the paint is dry, spray the bangle with a glossy sealant.

3. Leaving a small tail of thread, begin wrapping the bangle with the crewel thread, covering the tail as you wrap to secure it. Continue wrapping until you've covered about a quarter of the bangle. Make sure not to overlap the thread; keep it nice and smooth to achieve an even look.

4. To change colours, tie a knot in the current thread with a new colour. Trim off the first colour of thread, leaving a 12mm (½in) tail end. Continue to wrap with the new colour, covering the ends of threads as you work.

5. Wrap the thread until you have covered over half of the bangle, changing the colours as you go. To finish, loop the thread around itself and tie a knot. Thread the end through the needle and run the thread through 2.5cm (1in) of the wrapped thread on the inside of the bangle. Pull the thread tight and clip the end close to the bangle.

TIP

These bangles would also be pretty if you left the wood unfinished. I would still recommend using a sealant before you begin wrapping the thread to protect the wood from being scuffed over time.

mini masterpiece necklace

Who needs to take a trip to the museum when you can wear a miniature version of your favourite artwork anytime? This darling necklace is the perfect way to highlight your favourite artist and show off your fabulous style at the same time. This project has special meaning for me – the artist who created my necklace artwork is my dad. He is an amazing watercolourist and has always been a huge inspiration to me. Thank you, Dad!

INSTRUCTIONS

1. Cut out the fabric and greaseproof paper to the given dimensions. Place the greaseproof paper, shiny side up, on the ironing board and lay the fabric over it. Iron the fabric to the paper. Trim the fabric and paper to 21.5 × 28cm (8½ × 11in).

2. Size the artwork to 4.5 × 6cm (1¾ × 2¼in) or just a little larger than the opening of the frame. Place your fabric in the printer and print the image onto the fabric. It helps to set your printer to a special paper setting. Trim around your artwork and remove the greaseproof paper backing.

3. Place the design behind the opening in the frame. Use embroidery thread to stitch the fabric to the frame through the holes that edge the opening. If the frame doesn't have holes, glue the fabric to the back instead.

4. Place a piece of heavyweight stabiliser behind the fabric to make sure it doesn't become distorted over time, then position the felt piece over the back. Glue in place with jewellery glue.

5. Finish by adding the smaller jump ring to the top of the frame. Feed the chain through the ring and add the closure with the two larger jump rings and lobster clasp.

MATERIALS

Wooden necklace frame – sample measures 6.2 × 7cm (2½ × 2¾in)

23 × 30.5cm (9 × 12in) piece of heavyweight white fabric

23 × 30.5cm (9 × 12in) piece of greaseproof paper

Image for printing

4 × 6.5cm (1½ × 2½in) heavyweight stabiliser

6 × 6.5cm (2¼ × 2½in) piece of felt

Embroidery thread

2 × 9mm jump rings

7mm jump ring

Lobster clasp

71cm (28in) length of gold chain

Jewellery glue

EQUIPMENT

Scissors

Needle

Inkjet printer

Iron

Flat nose pliers

micro bead ring

Simple costume rings are such fun to make with friends; it's so easy to gather up supplies, sit around a table and create with others. You can make a wide variety of styles and projects from just one collection of materials. Craft parties are one of my favourite types of get-togethers – who doesn't love the chance to make things, eat yummy snacks and chat with friends, all at the same time?

MATERIALS

Button with an inverted, curved top

Circular ring blank, slightly smaller than the button

Micro beads

Jewellery glue

Mod Podge Dimensional Magic

EQUIPMENT

Wire cutters

INSTRUCTIONS

1. If the button has a shank, use the wire cutters to remove it as close to the button as possible. If the button doesn't have a shank, place it on a piece of parchment paper and fill each of the holes in the centre with jewellery glue to seal them off. Wait until mostly dry before moving on to the next step.

2. Place the button on a flat, covered surface – a baking sheet works well here because it will catch any extra micro beads. Fill the curved area with a layer of Dimensional Magic – you don't want to add so much that the product starts to dome, just aim for a nice, flat layer.

3. Pour the micro beads very slowly over the face of the button, adding enough to cover the Dimensional Magic in a smooth layer. Tap down any beads that are layered on top of each other and wipe off any Dimensional Magic that spreads up the sides of the button.

4. Let the Dimensional Magic set a little, then press the beads further into the product. Tilt the button slightly to shake off any loose beads.

5. When the beads are set in place, secure a ring blank to the back of the button with jewellery glue.

porcelain piece necklace

If you have ever broken a favourite dish or teacup, you know how frustrating it is to throw those pieces away. Now you can give new life to broken crockery with this pretty porcelain necklace. You don't have to know complex jewellery skills or soldering either – all you need is sandpaper and some paint.

MATERIALS

Broken piece of china (or a dish you don't mind breaking)

Heavy grit sandpaper, or handheld rotary tool with sanding attachment

Silver leaf paint pen

Flat back bail

2 × 4mm jump rings

9mm jump ring

Lobster clasp

56cm (22in) length of silver chain

EQUIPMENT

Flat nose pliers

Round nose pliers

Wire cutters

Optional: hammer and towel

INSTRUCTIONS

1. If you don't already have broken pieces of china, choose a plate you like that has a pretty pattern. Place the dish in a towel and use a hammer to lightly break it. Be careful when doing this and make sure you wear protective glasses. Check the pieces of your plate. If you need to make them a little smaller, break up the pieces further.

2. To remove the rough edges of the piece you are using, sand the piece with heavy grit sandpaper until the edges are completely smooth to the touch. You can also use a sanding attachment on a rotary tool.

3. Once the edges are smooth, clean the piece off with a damp cloth. Paint the sides and back of the porcelain piece with the silver leaf paint pen.

4. Glue the flat back bail to the top, reverse side of the porcelain piece. Finish the necklace by feeding a chain through the loop on the bail and adding the jump rings and a lobster clasp to the ends of the chain.

TIPS

You can also find broken pieces of china online, or search your local charity shops for dishes and china you don't mind smashing.

rings and beads bracelet

A stretch bracelet is such a wonderful project for beginners. Simple to make and fun to customise, this sweet bracelet is a mixture of chunky chains and colourful beads, making it the perfect little accessory to dress up any casual outfit. They are so quick to assemble, you could make a whole armful to wear in thirty minutes. Wouldn't a bracelet with ombré beads be so pretty? Or maybe even a strand of pearls with a rose gold chain?

MATERIALS

30.5cm (12in) length of 1mm elastic cord

11.5cm (4½in) long strand of beads

30.5cm (12in) length of large open chain

Jewellery glue

EQUIPMENT

Scissors

Wire cutters or pliers to separate chain

INSTRUCTIONS

1. Cut with wire cutters, or use pliers to open the links of chain, creating two separate strands of chain each measuring 15cm (6in) long.

2. Feed the length of elastic cord through each link of one of the chain lengths. The chain should gather up to create the look of jumbled links.

3. Add 6cm (2¼in) of beads to the elastic cord.

4. Repeat the last two steps with the second length of chain and the remaining 6cm (2¼in) of beads.

5. Pull the two ends of the elastic cord up so the elastic is pulled tight but isn't stretched. Knot the ends with a surgeon's knot (see page 121). Secure the knot with a small dot of jewellery glue and leave to dry.

TIP

These measurements create an 18cm (7in) stretch bracelet, but you can easily adjust the measurement by adding or removing beads or chain. Change the design by interspersing the chain sections with beads at more regular intervals, or even try an all chain version!

map bangle

This bangle is perfect for the traveller in your life. It's great as a 'bon voyage' gift or it would be perfect as a keepsake from a special holiday. Can't decide where in the world you like best? Use the whole world map, like I did!

INSTRUCTIONS

1. Paint the inner section of the bangle, taking the paint along the top and bottom edges and just onto the outside of the bangle.

2. Begin tearing sections of the map. You should aim for irregular, "square-ish" pieces measuring approximately ½–1 in (1.2–2.5 cm) across. Brush the back of a map piece with decoupage, and lay it over the outside of the bangle. Press the piece in place and remove any creases. Repeat with more of the map paper pieces, mixing up the colours and overlapping the tear-outs so the bangle doesn't show through. Cover as much of the front of the bangle as you can, taking the paper right up to the top and bottom edges.

3. Once the map pieces are mostly dry, paint the bangle with the red shimmer paint pen, covering the top and bottom edges and down onto the front in any places where the map doesn't quite reach the edge. This will give the piece an antiqued look.

4. Once everything is dry, cover the bangle with another coat of decoupage to seal it.

MATERIALS

Unfinished spiral wood bangle

Craft paint in a colour that coordinates with your map

Satin decoupage

Map paper

Red shimmer paint pen

EQUIPMENT

Paintbrush

TIP

Create a similar bangle without tearing and overlapping the map pieces for a bracelet that highlights a full section of a map. I recommend choosing a bangle with a smoother front edge than the one shown in the sample, as this will prevent the paper from wrinkling as you decoupage over it.

fabric and leather watch

Do you ever save special pieces of fabric for just the right project? I do, all the time. This watch cuff is perfect for showcasing a precious piece of fabric, so start pulling out your favourites.

MATERIALS

Blank leather cuff with snap fastening

Watch face with two loops at top and bottom

25cm (5in) square piece of fabric

Sewing thread to match fabric

EQUIPMENT

Sewing machine

Iron

Scissors

INSTRUCTIONS

1. Cut the fabric into two strips measuring 6.5 x 12.5cm (2½ x 5in) each. Fold each fabric strip in half lengthways so the right sides are together.

2. Stitch each fabric strip into a tube by sewing along the long side, 6mm (¼in) from the raw edge. Repeat for the second strip. Turn both tubes inside out and press, so the seam is at the centre of the tube.

3. Place the watch face in the centre of the leather cuff. Fold one fabric piece over the loop at the bottom of the watch face, then fold the fabric end under one more time. Stitch across the fabric strip, just above the folded edge, sewing through the leather at the same time. If the leather is struggling to go through the machine, place tissue paper above and below the leather piece to allow it to move smoothly through the machine, then remove the tissue paper once you have finished sewing.

4. Fold the end of the fabric strip under twice, just above the snap on the bottom of the cuff. Stitch the fabric to the leather at each end with a rectangle shape.

5. Repeat for the second fabric strip at the top of the leather piece with the top loop of the watch face to finish off the cuff.

TIP

If you cannot find a leather blank, it's simple to make your own. Cut a piece of leather in the width and length you'd like and add a snap fastener at each end.

rhinestone wrapped earrings

These little post earrings are so easy to customise. They can be made with almost any bead that has a flat section on one side, and they would be cute with a contrasting coloured rhinestone strand wrapped around the bead, too. Wouldn't a white crystal bead edged with turquoise rhinestones be so fun? There really are so many options with this design.

MATERIALS

2 beads with a flat or semi-flat section at the back

Rhinestone strand, long enough to wrap around both beads

Flat front post earrings and backs

Jewellery glue

EQUIPMENT

Wire cutters

Tape measure

INSTRUCTIONS

1. Measure out the area of the bead you would like the rhinestone strand to wrap around and cut two equal lengths from the strand.

2. Glue the rhinestone strands in place around each bead, so the sides of the rhinestones are glued to the bead and not the bases, to ensure the stones will show when the earrings are worn. Hold the strands in place until the glue has set and the stones are secure.

3. Once thoroughly dry, glue the earring post to the back of the bead. Make sure to glue the posts at the same place on each bead or the earrings will look different when they are worn.

TIP

It would be very easy to create a hanging drop version of these earrings. Begin by placing the bead on a head pin and create a loop at the top. Glue the rhinestone strand along the side edge of the bead, starting and finishing on either side of the pin loop. Once the glue is dry, add the loops to a set of ear wires and you're all finished!

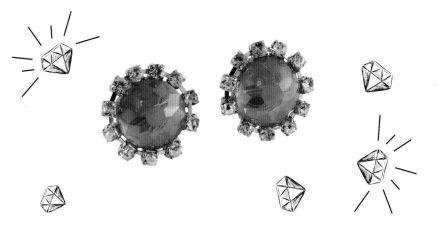

time for tea ring

This is really more like a five-minute project, which I love. Sometimes we just need to create something very cute in a very short amount of time! It is the perfect accessory when you are looking for something sweet to wear – maybe to an afternoon tea party or a trip to the antique shop.

MATERIALS

Miniature teacup

Miniature plate

13mm circle-based ring blank

Jewellery glue

INSTRUCTIONS

1. Glue the teacup to the plate and leave to dry.

2. Glue the plate to the ring and set upright to dry. Make sure the teacup is centred and facing the right way on the base.

TIP

If you are having trouble finding tiny crockery pieces similar to the sample, you can always check online, but another great source is the miniature section of your local craft or hobby shop. This cup and plate came as part of a little dinner table set for a dollhouse. The great thing about buying them this way is you then have several pieces to create multiple rings as favours for your next party!

daisy earrings

If you have been wanting to try your hand at embroidery, these little daisies are the perfect project to start with. They are made up with very simple stitches and are such a great gift idea, too. See pages 122–124 for help with embroidery techniques.

INSTRUCTIONS

1. Place the fabric in the embroidery hoop. Trace the two glass domes onto the fabric with the disappearing ink marker, making sure to leave at least 2.5cm (1in) between the ovals. Trace the daisy pattern (see page 125) in the centre of the ovals.

2. Embroider the design using a lazy daisy stitch for the flower petals and leaves, a backstitch for the stem and a French knot for the centre of the flower (see pages 122–124).

3. Remove the fabric from the hoop and cut around the design, leaving at least 12mm (½in) all around the oval shape. Use a damp cloth to remove any marker on the fabric.

4. Brush a light coat of decoupage over the glass dome. Lay the embroidered fabric over the dome, making sure to centre the design. Fold the fabric over the dome and around to the back and pull it tight, without distorting the design. Add more decoupage to the back of the dome to glue down the fabric on the reverse side.

5. Once the decoupage is set up, add jewellery glue to the gem settings. Place the embroidery pieces into the setting and fold the prongs in around the domes using pliers.

6. Open up the rings at the base of the ear wires and add the loops on the settings. Close the rings.

MATERIALS

12.5cm (5in) square of fabric

7.5cm (3in) embroidery hoop

Embroidery thread in white, gold and green

Decoupage

Disappearing ink marker

2 × clear glass domes – 13 × 18mm

2 × antique brass gem prong settings with top loop – 13 × 18mm

2 × ear wires

Jewellery glue

EQUIPMENT

Embroidery needle

Flat nose pliers

Scissors

Paintbrush

INTERMEDIATE

projects

braided leather bracelet

This bracelet is so easy to make and would be perfect for a crafty girls' night in. You could pick up all the findings, plus an assortment of connector charms and leather cording, so your guests can mix and match styles and colours to suit their own look. This project is simple enough that you and your friends could make a few while watching a movie or snacking on appetisers.

INSTRUCTIONS

1. Begin by cutting three strands of leather cording, each measuring 30.5cm (12in). Place one end of each of the strands side-by-side in a ribbon clamp. Use the flat nose pliers to close the clamp around the cording.

2. Braid the cording until it is the desired length for your bracelet. For a bracelet with a finished measurement of 18cm (7in), as shown here, cut the cording braid at 16.5cm (6½in) to allow for the 12mm (½in) length of the fastenings.

3. Secure and finish off the end of the braided cording with the second ribbon clamp.

4. Use the needle and thread to stitch the connector charm to the centre front of the bracelet, keeping your stitches as small as possible.

5. Finish off the bracelet by adding a 6mm jump ring to the loops on each of the ribbon clamps. Add a lobster clasp to one jump ring and the 9mm jump ring to the other.

MATERIALS

91.5cm (36in) length of leather cording, decorated with small studs (or plain leather cording)

Connector charm with a ring at each end

Sewing thread to match the leather cording

2 × 2mm ribbon end clamps

2 × 6mm jump rings

9mm jump ring

Lobster clasp

EQUIPMENT

Tape measure

Scissors

Flat nose pliers

Round nose pliers

Sewing needle

TIP

For a longer bracelet, add a 2.5–5cm (1–2in) length of small open link chain to the 9mm jump ring, and add a small bead or charm to the end of the chain. To fasten, you can then connect the lobster clasp anywhere along the chain for additional length.

wire wrapped geode necklace

Incorporating natural elements into your jewellery designs is a great way to create unique and eye-catching accessories. These geode slices are readily available in local bead shops and online. They come in a wide variety of gorgeous colours and sizes – just keep in mind that the larger the slice, the heavier the stone will be. Choose a neutral stone that you can wear with everything or a bright colour for a standout statement piece.

MATERIALS

Geode slice – sample measures about 35 × 80mm (1½ × 3in) with pre-drilled hole

Gold wrapping wire

Gold paint pen

10mm jump ring

71cm (28in) length of gold necklace chain

2 × 5mm jump rings

9mm jump ring

Lobster clasp

EQUIPMENT

Needle nose pliers

Flat nose pliers

Wire cutters

INSTRUCTIONS

1. Paint the sides of the geode with gold paint, taking the paint up onto the front and back faces slightly. Leave to dry.

2. Put the 10mm jump ring through the hole drilled at the top of the geode. Place one end of the wrapping wire a tiny way into the hole on the reverse side of the geode. Begin wrapping the wire around the top section of the geode, pulling the wire tight. Once you have a few wraps completed, wrap the wire tightly a couple times around one of the places where the wire crosses on the reverse side – this will hold the wire in place. Continue wrapping, crossing the wire over the front and reverse side and making small wraps on the reverse to hold the wire in place on the geode.

3. Once the geode is wrapped, finish by wrapping the end of the wire a few times around a place on the reverse side where the wires cross. Pull the wire tight and cut close to the wrapping with wire cutters. If necessary, bend the end of the wire in with needle nose pliers.

4. Feed the necklace chain through the large jump ring and finish the chain with the 5mm jump rings and the lobster clasp.

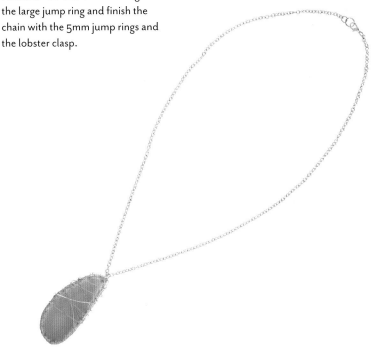

feather and chain earrings

These earrings add so much style to your wardrobe. You can create many different looks with this project, just by changing the colour of the leather and the types of beads that hang from the chains. This black and gold version is just a little glamorous. You could also make a turquoise and coral set inspired by the Aztec look.

MATERIALS

7.5cm (3in) square of leather

2 × 5mm eyelets

4 × 6mm beads

4 × head pins

23cm (9in) length of gold chain

2 × 9mm jump rings

2 × ear wires

Jewellery glue

EQUIPMENT

Wire cutters

Flat nose pliers

Round nose pliers

Scissors

INSTRUCTIONS

1. Trace the feather pattern (see page 125). Use your pattern to cut out two feather shapes from the leather. Make sure you flip the template over for one of the feathers to make them mirror images of each other.

2. Cut a small hole in the top of the feather, at least 5mm (¼in) from the top. Add a small drop of jewellery glue to the hole and place the eyelet through the hole.

3. Add a 9mm jump ring to the eyelet. Cut the chain into two 11.5cm (4½in) lengths. Fold the chain in half, so one end is just a little longer than the other. Place the link at the top of the fold in the chain and through the jump ring as well.

4. Place the 6mm beads on the head pins and create a loop at the top of each bead. Add the loop above each of the beads to the bottom links of the chains.

5. Open the loop at the bottom of the ear wire, add the 9mm jump ring to the loop and close it.

6. Repeat for the second earring.

charm stretch bracelet

This simple bracelet is perfect for highlighting colourful or unique beads. The sweet little rhinestone charms give just the right amount of sparkle to accentuate the beads. I fell in love with these blue and white beads, which have the look of a blue willow pattern. Any style of beads would be fun here, though – whether it's bright florals, a wooden assortment, or even a simple strand of pearls. There are just so many options with this easy stretch bracelet.

MATERIALS

30.5cm (12in) length of 1mm elastic cord

16 8mm beads

5 × 12mm beads
(or an 18cm (7in) length of any size beads)

6 × 9mm jump rings

6 × rhinestone charms with loops

Jewellery glue

EQUIPMENT

Scissors

Flat nose pliers

Round nose pliers

INSTRUCTIONS

1. Add a rhinestone charm to each of the 9mm jump rings. If you are unable to find rhinestones or other charms you like, you can create your own by adding small crystals to head pins and forming a loop at the top of the crystal.

2. String the beads onto the elastic cord as follows: start by adding eight of the smaller 8mm beads, place a rhinestone charm jump ring next, then a larger 12mm bead. Continue alternating the rhinestone charm jump rings and 12mm beads until you reach the last jump ring. Make sure all the charms face the same direction.

3. Add the remaining 8mm beads to the strand.

4. Pull the two ends of the elastic cord up so the cord is pulled tight but isn't stretched. Knot the ends with a surgeon's knot (see page 121). Secure the knot with a small dot of jewellery glue and leave to dry.

vintage ribbon and beads necklace

This unique necklace is the perfect accessory to show off a pretty and colourful length of ribbon. The vintage ribbon used here has been paired with some fun, open metal beads, but almost any style of bead would look just as great.

MATERIALS

91.5cm (36in) length of 12mm (½in) wide ribbon

28cm (11in) length of 1mm gold chain

2 × chain connectors

18 × 3mm crimp beads

2 × 9mm jump rings

16 × beads, 10 × 16mm, or 29cm (11½in) length of any size beads

Thread to match ribbon

EQUIPMENT

Round nose pliers

Flat nose pliers

Wire cutters

Crimp pliers

Needle

INSTRUCTIONS

1. Add a connector clamp to one end of the gold chain. Add a crimp bead, but do not clamp it to the chain. Add a large bead then continue alternating crimp beads and large beads until you have strung 14 large beads, or 24cm (9½in) of beads, onto the ribbon.

2. String a crimp bead and crimp it in place. Leave a 10mm (½in) space then add another crimp bead. Crimp in place. Add two more large beads and crimp beads, alternating as before. Finish the chain with another connector clamp.

3. Add each of the connector clamps to a 9mm jump ring.

4. Cut a 46cm (18 in) length of ribbon. Feed one end through the right hand jump ring and fold the end of the ribbon over twice on the reverse side to create a hem. Stitch the end in place for a neat finish.

5. Repeat for the other end of the ribbon and the left hand 9mm jump ring – make sure the ribbon isn't twisted before stitching it down.

6. Tie the remaining length of ribbon in a small bow. Place the bow over the open section in the thin chain. Stitch the bow in place around the chain on the reverse side of the bow with small stitches.

7. Hem the ends of the bow so the raw edges do not show. This will prevent your ribbon from fraying.

lace drop earrings

These lace earrings have such a classic, delicate style. They look beautiful in this neutral palette, decorated with cream and white for a vintage look. You could create a more modern pair of earrings by changing the lace colour at the back and adding a bright bead at the bottom, or decoupage a bright floral fabric on the back. There are so many options with this design.

INSTRUCTIONS

1. Place the clear glass bead onto the lace. Trim a lace piece to the same size as the bead. Don't completely cover the bead to the bottom – you want a little of the glass showing through at the base of the bead.

2. Brush a thin layer of decoupage over the lace. Place the lace on the reverse side of the bead. When mostly dry, add a second coat of decoupage over the lace.

3. Place the pearl on a head pin and form a loop at the top. Add this loop to the bottom loop of the glass bead.

4. Add a jump ring to the top loop of the glass bead. Add this jump ring to the bottom loop of the ear wire.

5. Repeat for the second earring.

MATERIALS

2 × clear faceted glass beads with a loop at each end

2 × 6mm pearls

2 × head pins

2 × 5mm jump rings

2 × ear wires

2.5 × 5cm (1 × 2in) piece of thin nylon lace

Glossy decoupage

EQUIPMENT

Round nose pliers

Flat nose pliers

Wire cutters

Scissors

Paintbrush

INTERMEDIATE

peaches and cream necklace

A statement necklace is a great way to finish off an outfit or to dress-up a casual T-shirt and jeans. This necklace is just a simple strand of beads, but you can mix and match fun unique beads for an accessory that is really creative and pretty.

INSTRUCTIONS

1. Place a crimp bead on one end of the wire. Loop the wire through a closed 6mm jump ring and then back through the crimp bead. The short end of the wire should be approximately 2.5cm (1in) long. Crimp the bead closed.

2. Lay the beads out on a bead tray to determine the design. Keep the smallest beads towards the ends of the necklace, and place the largest beads at the centre.

3. Begin stringing the smallest beads onto the wire, making sure to cover the short end of the wire as you go. Continue stringing until all the beads are on the wire.

4. Add a crimp bead to the wire. Loop the wire through a closed 6mm jump ring then back through the crimp bead. Feed the wire through approximately 2.5cm (1in) of the beads on the wire. Pull the strand up so the beads are all touching, without pulling so tight that the necklace doesn't lay straight.

5. Crimp the bead closed and trim the wire with wire cutters. Finish the necklace by adding the 9mm jump ring to one of the smaller jump rings and the lobster clasp to the other.

MATERIALS

Assortment of beads – choose beads that graduate in size, with the largest beads being at the centre of the necklace

71cm (28in) length of beading wire to make a 61cm (24in) necklace

2 × crimp beads

2 × 6mm jump rings

9mm jump ring

Lobster clasp

EQUIPMENT

Needle nose pliers

Flat nose pliers

Wire cutters

Crimping pliers

Bead tray

embroidered monogram ring

This embroidered monogram ring is such a pretty accessory and would make a wonderful gift. It is easy to find a letter design to use – simply look through fonts to choose a style you like, then trace the letter onto the fabric. Finish by adding a simple flower in a contrasting colour, or leave the design plain. See pages 122–124 for help with embroidery techniques.

MATERIALS

20mm ring blank with setting base

20mm round glass cabochon

Small amount of fabric – enough to fit in an embroidery hoop

Disappearing ink marker

Embroidery hoop

Embroidery thread

Decoupage

Jewellery glue

EQUIPMENT

Scissors

Embroidery needle

Paintbrush

INSTRUCTIONS

1. Place the fabric in the embroidery hoop. Trace around the outside of the glass cabochon with the marker. Trace or draw the desired design in the middle of the circle, leaving some space around the outer edge.

2. Embroider the design. Letters look great with a simple backstitch and flowers can easily be made with a backstitch stem and little French knots for the flower heads (see page 123).

3. Remove the fabric from the hoop. Cut a circle around the design, approximately 2cm (¾in) outside of the marker circle. Blot the fabric with a damp cloth to remove any marker lines.

4. Brush the outer dome of the glass cabochon with a light coat of decoupage. Lay the fabric over the dome. Add more decoupage to the back edges and wrap the fabric around to the back of the glass. As the fabric dries, continue wrapping the fabric tightly and folding the edges over one another at the back until the fabric is as flat as possible. Leave the decoupage to dry for a short while.

5. Put a layer of jewellery glue in the ring setting. Place the embroidered piece in the setting, adjusting it lightly to make sure the design is aligned correctly.

pearl drop earrings

There are so many style options with these cute earrings. You can easily substitute the drop beads if you don't want to use pearls – as long as the beads fit within the hoops, they will work.

INSTRUCTIONS

1. Place an eye pin through a round bead. Form a loop at the other end.

2. Add a teardrop pearl bead to a head pin and form a loop at the top.

3. Open up a 9mm jump ring and add the loop of an eye pin onto a round bead, the loop of a pearl bead and an oval hoop. Close the ring. When you hang the earring from the bead, the hoop and pearl bead will fall to the bottom of the jump ring.

4. Add the other loop on the round bead eye pin to a kidney ear wire, moving the loop until it sits in the bottom open loop of the ear wire. Close the open loop as much as possible with round nose pliers without distorting the shape of the ear wire.

5. Repeat for the second earring.

TIP

You could also create a two tier version for a longer style by adding another drop bead to a head pin and creating a loop at the top. Add the loop to a 9mm jump ring along with another hoop, then add the jump ring to the bottom of the first hoop, and you have a fun double hoop set of earrings.

MATERIALS

2 × 7mm round beads

2 × 13mm long teardrop pearl beads

2 × 12 × 24mm (½ × 1in) gold oval hoops

2 × eye pins

2 × head pins

2 × 9mm jump rings

2 × small gold kidney ear wires

EQUIPMENT

Wire cutters

Round nose pliers

Flat nose pliers

bright chain cuff

Bring on the colour! This darling cuff is all dressed up with a bright enamel chain and some gorgeous chiffon flowers in coordinating colours. It looks complicated but is so simple to make – your friends will be begging to know where you bought it.

INSTRUCTIONS

1. Wrap the chain around the circumference of the cuff bracelet to determine the length required – it should completely wrap around the centre without overlapping. Cut the chain to fit accordingly. Using jewellery glue, glue the chain in place along the centre of the cuff.

2. To create each of the flowers, fold the strip of fabric in half, so the long edges meet and the fabric forms a tube. Thread your needle with coordinating thread and knot the end. Sew a running stitch along the bottom edge, gathering the fabric up as you go (see page 122). When the fabric is approximately 7.5cm (3in) long, knot the thread and cut it.

3. Cut a small 12mm (½in) circle of felt to match the fabric. Roll the fabric up into a spiral and use the hot glue to join the base of the flower to the felt. Gently pull the fabric open to create a flower and glue a rhinestone to the centre. Repeat to make as many flowers as you would like on your bracelet.

4. Use jewellery glue to stick the flowers onto the wooden bangle, covering up the section where the enamel chain meets.

MATERIALS

Stained wooden cuff bracelet

30.5cm (12in) length of chunky enamel chain

Assorted lightweight fabrics – 5 × 23cm (2 × 9in) strip for each flower

Felt

Hot glue

6 × rhinestones in settings

Jewellery glue

Sewing thread to match fabrics

EQUIPMENT

Wire cutters

Needle

Hot glue gun

TIP

If you cannot find a pre-stained cuff, most craft shops and several online suppliers sell unfinished wooden bangles. Use a stain and glossy sealant on the unfinished wood and you are all ready to go.

leather chevron necklace

Leather and fabric make a perfect combination, and this necklace is a beautiful way to mix and match some pretty fabrics and leather scraps.

INSTRUCTIONS

1. Cut out the leather chevron pieces by tracing the pattern on page 125.

2. Iron the fusible webbing to the back of the fabric pieces. Cut out the fabric chevrons to the same shape as the leather chevrons, but 5mm (¼in) smaller. Remove the paper backing from the fusible webbing.

3. Lay the fabric over the leather and cover with an ironing cloth. Lightly iron the fabric in place onto the leather, but be careful not to use too much pressure – you don't want the leather to get overly hot.

4. With a sewing machine, stitch each of the fabric pieces in place just inside the edges of the fabric.

5. Cut out three pieces of felt, each a little smaller than the leather pieces.

6. Stitch a jump ring to the top of each of the felt pieces, 5mm (¼in) in from each side. On two of the felt pieces, stitch a jump ring at the bottom, 5mm (¼in) from each side; the jump rings should be 3mm (⅛in) from the top and bottom of the felt, so half of the ring is visible above the felt.

7. Turn the felt pieces so the stitching is on the inside. Place the felt onto the wrong side of the leather pieces and glue the felt in place.

8. Place each of the small beads onto an eye ring and form a loop at the other end.

9. Take the chevron piece with only two jump rings in the top of it, place it at the bottom and connect it to the middle leather piece by positioning the beads between the jump rings. Repeat for the middle and top leather pieces.

10. Divide the chain into two 28cm (11in) lengths. Add each of the chain pieces to the eye loop beads above the top piece of leather. Finish the necklace by adding a lobster clasp to one side. If the chain doesn't have large enough links, add a jump ring as well.

MATERIALS

7.5 × 10cm (3 × 4in) piece of leather

3 pieces of fabric – 2.5 × 6.5cm (1 × 2½in)

Fusible webbing

Thread to match fabric and felt

7.5 × 10cm (3 × 4in) piece of felt to match leather

10 × 7mm jump rings

6 × eye pins

6 × 6mm beads

56cm (22in) length of medium chain

Lobster clasp

Jewellery glue

EQUIPMENT

Sewing machine

Wire cutters

Round nose pliers

Flat nose pliers

Needle

INTERMEDIATE

thread wrapped earrings

Wrapping decorative pieces in embroidery thread is such an easy and inexpensive way to add a little colour and texture to your jewellery designs. Consider mixing and matching your thread and bead colours, or even use variegated thread for some really interesting colour patterns in the wrapping.

INTERMEDIATE

MATERIALS

2 × brass geometric blanks – sample measures 10 × 30mm with a hole at the top

2 × 10mm beads

2 × eye pins

Embroidery thread

2 × ear wires

EQUIPMENT

Embroidery needle

Flat nose pliers

Round nose pliers

Scissors

INSTRUCTIONS

1. Cut a 20.5cm (8in) length of embroidery thread and thread it through the needle. Begin wrapping the thread around one of the brass geometric blanks, starting at the bottom and working your way upwards to the top, making sure to cover the loose end of the thread as you wrap. When you have wrapped approximately 12mm (½in) of the blank, pass the needle through the thread on the reverse side of the blank from the top to halfway down and pull tight. Trim the thread close to the blank.

2. Place the bead on the eye pin and form a loop at the top. Open the loop at the bottom of the bead and add the geometric blank, then close. Add the loop at the top of the bead to the loop on the ear wire.

3. Repeat for the second earring, making sure that the wrapping measures the same as on the first blank.

TIP

If you are having trouble keeping the thread in place on the diagonal lines of the geometric blank, add a tiny amount of jewellery glue on the reverse side of the blank to help keep everything secure.

clay bow necklace

Polymer clay is such an easy and fun medium to work with, and there are so many creative ways to make jewellery from it. This simple bow necklace is so charming, and it makes a wonderful piece to start with if you have never worked with clay before.

INTERMEDIATE

INSTRUCTIONS

1. Break off a medium-sized piece of clay and work it in your hands until it is soft and pliable. Divide the clay into two pieces.

2. Roll one of the pieces into a long, narrow strip, approximately 6mm (¼in) thick, 12mm (½in) wide and 7.5cm (3in) long. Fold the two short ends towards the centre of the strip and pinch lightly together to form the top of the bow. Place the pencil or drinking straw in the loops of the bow and raise up the sections so the bow shape is nicely rounded.

3. Create another strip of clay the same size. Cut a triangle out of each end of the strip to form the bottoms of the ribbon. Bend the ends towards each other to form an upside down "V" shape. Press the top of the V to the back centre section of the bow loops. Be careful not to crease or leave fingerprints in the clay. Using the point of a pencil or wire, create a hole on the reverse side of each of the loops for the jump rings. Make sure the hole is large enough for the rings to easily fit through.

4. Bake the clay according to the directions on the packaging.

5. Once the clay has cooled, take the strip of fabric and fold the long edges of the strip in, wrapping the fabric around the centre of the bow. Fold the end of the fabric under on the back of the ribbon and stitch in place.

6. Place the 9mm jump rings through the holes on the back of the bow loops. Cut the chain in half and add each section to a jump ring. Add a 6mm jump ring to each end of the chain, then add the toggle closure pieces.

MATERIALS

Polymer clay

2 × 4cm (¾ × 1½in) piece of fabric

2 × 9mm jump rings

2 × 6mm jump rings

Toggle closure

51cm (20in) length of gold chain

Thread to match the fabric

EQUIPMENT

Pencil or drinking straw

Oven

Round nose pliers

Flat nose pliers

Wire cutters

Needle

acrylic dangle earrings

These earrings have such a fun retro vibe, but if that really isn't your thing, you could easily change the style by substituting the acrylic versions shown here for any drop or oval beads instead. The oversized kidney style ear wires really add to the overall look of the design, but if you want a shorter version they would be just as great using normal ear wires, or even a smaller kidney style set.

MATERIALS

4 × acrylic teardrop beads

4 × 8mm gold jump rings

2 × 5mm gold jump rings

7.5cm (3in) length of gold chain with small links

2 × large gold kidney ear wires

EQUIPMENT

Tape measure

Wire cutters

Round nose pliers

Flat nose pliers

INSTRUCTIONS

1. Begin by cutting four lengths of gold chain: two lengths measuring 22mm (¾in) and two lengths measuring 15mm (⅔in).

2. Add an 8mm jump ring to each of the four acrylic beads, then add a length of chain to each of the rings and close them. If you are using two different styles of beads, make sure the shorter length of chain is attached to one style and the longer length is attached to the other style (unless you want the earrings to look different, which is great, too).

3. Add one short chain with bead and one long chain with bead to the 5mm jump ring and close the ring.

4. Feed the ring onto the kidney ear wire until it rests in the small open loop at the bottom. Close the loop with round nose pliers as much as you can without distorting the shape of the ear wire.

5. Repeat for the second earring.

cat's meow necklace

Sometimes you just want to wear something fun, and this sweet little kitty necklace is just that. It is so easy to make and is such a cute way to show your love for your furry friends.

INSTRUCTIONS

1. Trace the face pattern (see page 125) onto the fabric and place the fabric in the embroidery hoop. Embroider the eyes and nose with a simple backstitch, and make a small French knot at the top of the nose to complete the features (see page 123).

2. With the disappearing ink marker, draw a 5cm (2in) circle around the embroidery design. Cut out the circle – this will give you enough fabric to wrap around to the reverse side of the dome. Brush a very light layer of decoupage onto the front and sides of the cabochon and wrap the fabric around it, centring the face in the middle. Use the decoupage to glue the fabric around to the back as well – you want it to be snug, without any puckers.

3. Glue the metal bail in place on the wooden frame. Trace and cut out small ear shapes (see page 125) from the leather scraps. Cut slightly smaller ear shapes from the fabric and glue to the middle of the leather ears. Glue the completed ears in place on the back of the wooden frame at either side of the bail. Cut out a small circle of felt, slightly smaller than the back of the pendant, and glue in place on the back of the pendant.

4. Glue the cabochon inside the pendant base, making sure the face is aligned correctly.

5. Finish your necklace by adding a chain through the bail. Place jump rings at either end of the chain and add a lobster clasp to one of the jump rings to finish.

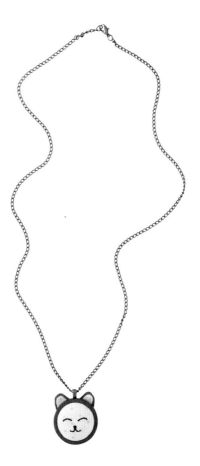

MATERIALS

Wooden frame with 3mm deep × 30mm diameter clear glass cabochon

15cm (6in) square of fabric

Disappearing ink marker

Embroidery hoop

Embroidery thread

2.5cm (1in) square of brown leather

5cm (2in) square of felt

Decoupage

Jewellery glue

Glue-on bail

71cm (28in) necklace chain

2 × 5mm jump rings

Lobster clasp

EQUIPMENT

Scissors

Needle nose pliers

Flat nose pliers

Embroidery needle

Paintbrush

INTERMEDIATE

cord and clasp bracelets

Do you remember making friendship bracelets at school? These updated versions are so much more stylish. Knotted bracelets are the perfect way to highlight a special connector bead or charm, and they look so sweet with their colourful cording. Although they are more fashionable than the bracelets we used to create, they still make perfect gifts for friends.

MATERIALS

Connector charm with a loop at each end

Thin jute cording in one or two colours per bracelet

Hook and eye cording ends

Jewellery glue

EQUIPMENT

Scissors

INTERMEDIATE

INSTRUCTIONS

1. For the two-colour bracelet, cut two strands of each colour of cording, each 61cm (24in) in length. Hold the strands together and fold all four in half. Feed the folded sections through one of the loops on the connector charm. Pull the twine through, then pass the ends through the small loop created to form a Lark's Head knot (see page 121). Pull the twine tight.

2. Place the connector under something heavy or pin it securely to a board to hold it in place as you tug on the piece and tie knots in it.

3. Begin an eight-strand chevron braid: hold four pieces of twine in each bundle – you should have two of colour A, then two of colour B in your left hand, with two of colour B and two of colour A in your right hand, so they are arranged AABB/BBAA.

4. Braid them as follows: take the far right strand and pass it over the three other right strands, placing it on the inside left. Take the far left strand, pass it over the other three left strands and place it on the inside right.

5. Continue as set in this way until you have braided 5.5cm (2¼in). Knot the end of the cording in an overhand knot (see page 121) and pull tight. Trim the ends of the cording to 6mm (¼in). Glue the ends into the eye end cap.

6. Repeat for the braid on the other side of the connector charm and the hook piece of the end cap.

pearl stacking rings

These sweet little rings take just a few minutes to make, and have such a pretty, feminine look to them. I made my set to fit as normal rings, but they would also look perfect worn higher on the finger as knuckle rings.

INSTRUCTIONS

1. Decide which finger you would like to wear the ring on. Wrap the wire around your finger so it crosses – you want it to fit, but not be so tight that you can't get the ring off!

2. Slip the wire off your finger and place the crimp bead on one side. Place the pearl on the other end of the wire and then feed that end of the wire through the crimp bead as well. You want the pearl at the top (where it would be on the front of the ring), and the wire crossed through the crimp bead on the bottom.

3. Place the ring back on your finger (or you can use a ring mandrel), and pull the ends of the wire so it tightens in place, again make sure not to make it too tight. Hold the ends of the wire in place, so the ring is the correct size, and slip it off your finger or mandrel.

4. Using the crimping pliers, crimp the bead in place at the back of the ring. Check that the wire is being held securely. Use wire cutters to trim off the ends of the wire as close as possible to the crimp bead. Make sure you don't have any sharp ends of wire. If you do, trim them a little more, or use the file to smooth them over.

5. Place the ring on a mandrel to make sure it is shaped nicely.

MATERIALS

12.5cm (5in) length of 22-gauge wire
2 × 1.5mm crimp beads
Small bead or pearl

EQUIPMENT

Crimping pliers
Wire cutters
Ring mandrel (optional)
Small file (optional)

TIP

For an additional design feature, add gold crimp beads onto either side of your pearl – this will prevent the pearl from slipping around and will also add a little more bling to your ring.

tassel chain earrings

These earrings are just perfect for a night out – they are so eye-catching during a party or dance. You can easily adjust the chain lengths: if you want to create a really glamorous version, cut even longer lengths, keeping the centre chain the longest, then cut each chain length a little shorter as you add them. Remember to buy a longer length of chain!

INTERMEDIATE

MATERIALS

2 × lever back ear wires

2 × eye pins

2 × 8mm crystal beads

2 × square jump rings

66cm (26in) length of small chain – links need to be large enough to fit over the square jump ring

EQUIPMENT

Wire cutters

Round nose pliers

Flat nose pliers

INSTRUCTIONS

1. Begin by cutting the lengths of chain. For two earrings you will need:

   2 × 38mm (1½in) lengths
   4 × 33mm (1¼in) lengths
   4 × 31mm (1⅛in) lengths
   4 × 29mm (1⅙in) lengths
   4 × 27mm (1in) lengths

2. Thread half of the chain pieces onto the square jump ring, starting with the shortest, moving to the longest, then back to the shortest. You will have a total of nine chain lengths on the jump ring. Close the jump ring.

3. Place the eye pin through the crystal bead and create a loop at the other end. Open one of the loops and add the top of the square jump ring – it will hang with a point at the top and one at the bottom.

4. Add the other eye loop to the ring on the lever back ear wire.

5. Repeat for the second earring.

TIP

To easily measure and match your lengths of chain, feed one end of a long piece of chain onto a piece of wire or a head pin. Hold the pin horizontally so the chain hangs freely. Cut to the desired measurement. Add the next piece of chain to the wire and you can easily match up lengths to the first piece of chain as they hang side-by-side.

beaded strand bracelet

A beaded strand bracelet is simple to make but gives you so many options for different styles, colours and looks – as many as there are different beads.

INSTRUCTIONS

1. Feed the beading wire through a crimp bead. Loop the wire around a closed jump ring, then back through the crimp bead and leave the short end 2.5cm (1in) long. Crimp the bead closed.

2. Begin stringing the beads, starting with the smallest first, working your way to the largest beads then back to the small beads, so the bead size increases then decreases. Make sure you cover the short end of the beading wire. You are aiming to have 18cm (7in) of beads on the wire.

3. Add a crimp bead to the wire and pass the wire through a large jump ring, back through the crimp bead, and then through approximately 2.5cm (1in) of the beads. Pull the wire tight and crimp the bead around the wire. Trim off any extra beading wire close to the beads with wire cutters.

4. Add a lobster clasp to the jump ring on the right-hand side of the bracelet.

5. Open up the teeth on the end clamp just a little. Fold the circle of fabric in half, then in half again. Place the folded point into the clamp and close the teeth of the clamp around the fabric with pliers.

6. Add the loop at the top of the end clamp to the smaller jump ring, also adding the 2.5cm (1in) of chain. Add a large jump ring to the other end of the chain. Add this jump ring to the ring at the left-hand side of the bracelet.

MATERIALS

25.5cm (10in) length of 0.30mm beading wire

2 × crimp beads

18cm (7in) length of graduating sizes bead strand

2 × 7mm jump rings

4mm jump ring

2.5cm (1in) length of silver chain

End clamp with teeth

2.5cm (1in) circle of fabric

Lobster clasp

EQUIPMENT

Wire cutters

Round nose pliers

Flat nose pliers

Crimp pliers

INTERMEDIATE

lace and pearl pendant

With its delicate vintage styling, this necklace makes the perfect accessory for a light summery dress or a flowing top. Pair it with a smaller colourful necklace or simple choker chain for added prettiness.

INSTRUCTIONS

1. Lay the lace medallion out on the parchment paper and try a few different configurations for the flowers and beads – place the resin flowers as the central focus, and decorate around the flowers with the smaller beads. Keep in mind you don't want anything too heavy on the lower section of the lace.

2. Glue the resin flowers in place. Once they are set, thread the sewing needle and knot the end. Begin stitching the small beads and pearls around the flowers. Sew the small charm below the resin flowers.

3. Sew or glue a few beads along the lower section of the lace, as desired, so they sit neatly with the lace design of the fabric. Make sure to keep the thread as invisible as possible and the knots at the back of the lace.

4. Glue the lace piece to the oval blank with jewellery glue, making sure you don't cover up the hole at the top of the blank.

5. Add a jump ring to the blank. Feed the chain through the jump ring. Finish the necklace by adding a jump ring to each end of the chain. On the right-hand side, add a lobster clasp to the jump ring.

MATERIALS

2.5 × 5cm (1 × 2in) lace medallion (cut from a piece of fabric or trim)

22 × 30mm antique brass oval blank with loop at top

2 × resin flowers

Small charm

Assorted small beads and pearls

Thread to match lace medallion

Jewellery glue

3 × 6mm jump rings

Lobster clasp

61cm (24in) length of chain

Parchment paper

EQUIPMENT

Wire cutters

Sewing needle

Round nose pliers

Flat nose pliers

ADVANCED

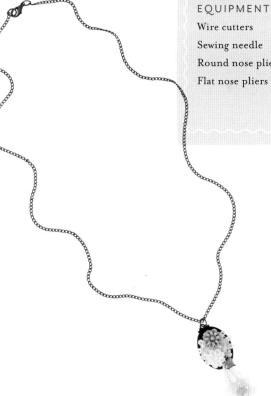

projects

colourful bar bracelet

Bar beads are a really fun way to create unique jewellery pieces. They come in a variety of materials: glass, metal, plastic, or ceramic; and all different sizes, too. Almost any size or style would work really well with this design.

INSTRUCTIONS

1. Cut two 22.5cm (10in) lengths of stringing wire. Feed a crimp bead onto one strand of wire. Run the wire through the left ring on the open loop connector. Crimp the bead closed. Repeat with the other length of stringing wire and a crimp bead on the right ring on the open loop piece.

2. Add a small crystal to each wire, making sure to cover the short end of the wire as well. String the two wires through the holes at each end of a glass bar bead.

3. Add another crystal to each of the wires, then another bar bead. Continue the pattern, alternating bars and crystals until you reach the last two crystals.

4. Add a crimp bead to each of the wires. Feed the wire through the loops on the other connector end piece. Pass the wires back through the crimp beads and a few of the crystals and bar beads.

5. Pull the wire tight and crimp the beads closed. Trim the end off the stringing wires.

6. Divide the lace into two 25.5cm (10in) lengths. Loop the end of one piece of lace through the open ring on the end piece. Fold the lace over and hand stitch it in place around the ring. Fold the other end of the lace over, just a little, and hem in place with small hand stitches. Repeat for the second length of lace on the other end piece.

7. Tie the lace in a bow around your wrist to wear.

MATERIALS

11 × glass bar beads, with two holes on each side

24 × 4mm crystal beads in assorted colours

2 × open loop connectors with two small loops on one side of the connector

4 × 1.3mm crimp beads

51cm (20in) length of 0.30mm bead stringing wire

51cm (20in) length of narrow lace trim

Thread to match lace

EQUIPMENT

Crimping pliers

Wire cutters

Sewing needle

Scissors

TIP

If you cannot source the loop connectors, you can switch these for decorative rings or jump rings. It would create a similar look and be just as simple to create.

ADVANCED

ombré crystal earrings

Ombré is an extremely striking effect, with its eye-catching colour changes from light to dark – it works well with everything, from furniture to clothing and even hairstyles. These earrings are so effective with their gradual change in colour. You are sure to receive compliments whenever you wear them!

INSTRUCTIONS

1. Place each of the beads on a head pin and form a loop at the top of each one. Separate the beads so you have 22 for each earring and lay them out with the colours going from the darkest to the lightest.

2. Cut the chain into two 2.5cm (1in) lengths. Begin adding the loops above the beads to the 2.5cm (1in) length of chain, starting at the bottom and working your way up towards the top. You want the chain to be completely covered and the colours to lighten gradually. You should have multiple loops on each link of chain.

3. Add the top link of the chain to the oval jump ring. Add the oval jump ring to the loop at the bottom of the decorative ear wire.

4. Repeat for the second earring. Make sure that the crystal beads are placed on the 2.5cm (1in) chain in the same order as the first earring so the colours lighten in the same places.

MATERIALS

44 × crystal beads in four graduated colours

44 × head pins

5cm (2in) length of medium-size chain

2 × oval jump rings – 6 × 8mm

2 × 30mm large decorative ear wires

EQUIPMENT

Wire cutters

Flat nose pliers

Round nose pliers

TIP

You might find it easier not to cut the chain until all the beads have been added – it will give you a little more length to hold on to as you are adding the beads. Make sure you keep each finished piece to 2.5cm (1in).

ADVANCED

beaded chandelier earrings

Chandelier earrings are a great way to create unique pieces of jewellery that look like you have put a ton of time into making them, but they can actually be created in just half an hour. These chandeliers have a pretty bar for loop beads built right in, but if you can't find these, any chandelier style will work. Just find one you like and decorate it with some beads and a pretty chain.

INSTRUCTIONS

1. Add two beads to the eye pins and create loops at the other end.

2. Add the remaining beads to the head pins and form loops at the top.

3. Cut four lengths of chain, measuring 4mm (⅛in) each. Add four of the beads to one end of each of the small chain pieces. Add the small jump rings to the other end of the chain.

4. Begin adding the beads to the loops along each chandelier piece. On the first, third and fifth loop, add the beads that only have head pins, opening the loops at the top of the bead and adding it to the loop on the chandelier. On the second and fourth loops, add the small jump rings that have the chains and beads attached.

5. Add the chandelier piece to one end of the bead that has the eye loops. Add the other eye loop to the decorative ear wire.

6. Repeat for the second earring.

MATERIALS

12 × 6mm round beads

2 × copper teardrop chandeliers with a central five-loop bar measuring 25 × 40mm (1 × 1½in)

10 × copper head pins

2 × copper eye pins

4 × 2mm copper jump rings

2.5cm (1in) length of copper chain

2 decorative copper ear wires

EQUIPMENT

Wire cutters

Round nose pliers

Flat nose pliers

ADVANCED

wrapped bead rings

Wire wrapping can be a little intimidating at first, but I encourage you to dive in. You've bought a whole spool of wire, so just keep practising with it. If you don't like your first run with a ring, snip off the wire and try again. I think you will find that after a few tries you will get a feel of how to bend the wire and will be ready to try more complicated projects.

MATERIALS

22-gauge wire

Gemstone – any stone bead will work well here, just choose one you like and that suits your finger

EQUIPMENT

Wire cutters

Round nose pliers

Ring mandrel

Small file (optional)

INSTRUCTIONS

1. Decide the size of the ring you want to make. If you aren't sure, find a ring that fits you well and slip it on the mandrel to determine its size.

2. Cut a length of wire approximately 51cm (20in) in length. Place the bead on the wire and position it at the centre.

3. Hold the bead against the mandrel at the size marking for the ring you're making. Wrap the wire to the back of the mandrel and cross the wires. Bring both ends around towards the front again.

4. Wrap the right-hand side up around the left-hand side of the stone, and wrap it around the stone and the wire twice.

5. Repeat with the left-hand side of the wire, wrapping opposite the right-hand side of the wire – if you wrapped that wire starting below the stone, wrap this one above the stone.

6. Gently remove the ring from the mandrel. Wrap the right-hand side wire around the ring wires, right up against the stone. It can help to hold the end of the wire with round nose pliers to pull it tight. Continue wrapping the wire around the ring so the loops of wire are tight and touching. Cut the wire after approximately seven wraps and bend the sharp end over – use a file to smooth them if necessary.

7. Wrap the left-hand side of the ring in the same way as the right.

TIP

If you don't have a ring mandrel, you can use anything round that is the size you would like your ring to be – a highlighter or paintbrush will work just as well.

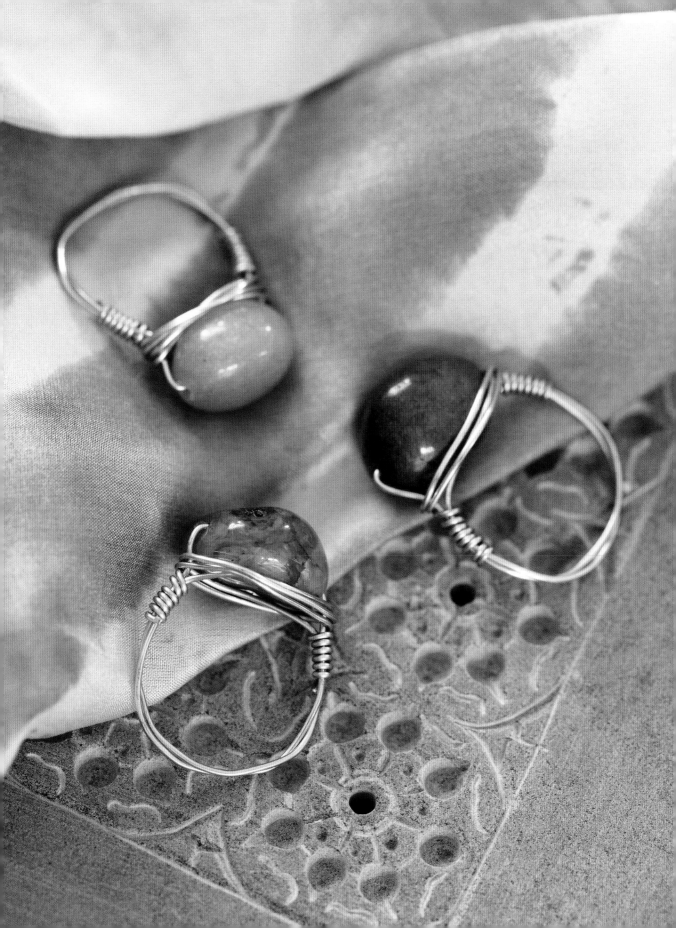

silver lining necklace

Even rainy days can be brightened up with this pretty necklace. The wooden cloud pendant is decorated with a row of sparkling crystal raindrops – they will catch the light every time you move and are sure to bring you lots of compliments.

INSTRUCTIONS

1. Paint the wooden cloud shape white and leave to dry.

2. While the cloud is drying, add the blue crystals to head pins and form loops. Cut seven pieces of chain, varying between 1.5–2cm (⅝–¾in) each. Add a crystal bead to the end link of each length of chain.

3. Cut a cloud shape out of the white felt, making it slightly smaller than the wooden shape. With the white thread, stitch the top links of the chains along the bottom edge of the cloud.

4. Once the wooden cloud is dry, thread the needle with three strands of silver embroidery thread. Sew diagonal stitches along the edge of the cloud shape using the drilled holes.

5. Add the 10mm jump ring to the top hole in the cloud. Glue the felt cloud shape to the back of the wooden one, so the silver chains hang along the bottom edge of the cloud.

6. Cut a 61cm (24in) length of silver chain and feed it through the jump ring at the top of the cloud.

7. Finish the necklace by adding the two small jump rings to each end of the chain. Add the 7mm jump ring to one side and the lobster clasp to the other.

MATERIALS

Wooden cloud pendant with pre-drilled holes

White paint

Silver embroidery thread

4 × 6.5cm (1½ × 2½in) piece of white felt

White sewing thread

76cm (30in) length of silver chain

7 × silver head pins

7 × 5mm assorted blue crystals

10mm jump ring

2 × 3mm jump rings

7mm jump ring

Lobster clasp

Jewellery glue

EQUIPMENT

Needle nose pliers

Flat nose pliers

Wire cutters

Needle

Paintbrush

Scissors

TIP

See page 128 for suppliers. You could also create a felt cloud shape by embroidering two felt cloud shapes together with silver thread and a blanket stitch (see page 124). Then attach the raindrops and necklace chains as per instructions.

fabric and rings bracelets

There are so many options with these cute bracelets – as many as there are fabric choices. The design looks so pretty on its own but is also great as a set. Stack them up and mix and match the fabrics and fixings for a bright pop of colour and style.

ADVANCED

INSTRUCTIONS

1. Wrap a piece of tape around one end of the cording and then 19cm (7½in) along. Cut the cording through the middle of the tape at the second tape marker – this will help to prevent it from fraying as you work. Feed the wire through the centre of the cording.

2. Wrap the fabric twice around the end of the cording. Add glue to one of the end caps and place the end of the fabric-covered cording in the cap. Hold in place until the glue has set.

3. Continue wrapping the fabric tightly around the cording until you reach the other end. Trim the fabric and add just a spot of glue to hold it in place.

4. Open a 9mm jump ring and wrap it around the cording, approximately 5cm (2in) from one end. Add a 12mm jump ring to the cording. Open the ring and feed it through the 9mm ring. Close it. This will prevent the rings from falling off the bracelet. Feed the remaining 12mm jump rings onto the cording.

5. Add a second 9mm ring approximately 5cm (2in) from the other end of the cording. Open the last 12mm ring and feed it through this 9mm ring to keep the rings in place at this end of the bracelet.

6. Add glue to the remaining end cap and place it on the other end of the cording.

7. Add a 6mm jump ring to one side with the closure clasp, then the 9mm jump ring to the other end.

MATERIALS

112cm (44in) length, 2.5cm (1in) strip of fabric

19cm (7½in) length of 6mm cording

2 × 8mm end caps with rings

Jewellery clasp

6mm jump ring

3 × 9mm jump ring

35 × 12mm jump rings

18cm (7in) length of thin gold wire

Jewellery glue

Clear tape

EQUIPMENT

Scissors

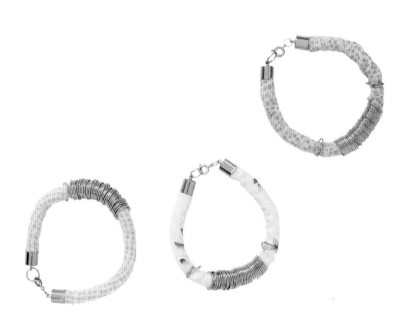

embroidered rose brooch

Attach this lovely brooch to your coat, scarf, or even your bag for a stylish and sweet accessory. It is the perfect way to bring a little of your garden with you wherever you go. See pages 122–124 for help with embroidery techniques.

INSTRUCTIONS

1. Trace the rose pattern (see page 125) onto another piece of paper. Now, trace the rose design onto your fabric with a disappearing ink marker.

2. Place the fabric in the embroidery hoop. For all parts of the design, work with three strands of embroidery thread. Use a stem stitch for the stem of the flower, lazy daisy stitch for the leaves, then add two small French knots at the top and bottom of the stem with light pink for the buds (see page 123).

3. Create the roses with a bullion stitch, using light pink for a few stitches in the centre of each rose, and use medium pink for the outer stitches in each of the roses (see page 124).

4. Remove the fabric from the hoop and remove any ink with a damp cloth. Trim the fabric to cover the front of the glass cabochon, allowing for a 12mm (½in) overhang.

5. Brush the front of the cabochon very lightly with decoupage. Lay the fabric over it and pull to the back of the glass oval. Brush decoupage around the back edge of the glass and pull the fabric around to the reverse side. Overlap the fabric on the back to avoid creasing around the edge. Hold in place until set.

6. Place a good layer of glue in the wooden base. Press the fabric-covered cabochon into the base and hold until set.

7. Glue the pin on the back of the wooden base.

MATERIALS

12.5cm (5in) square of light coloured fabric

7.5cm (3in) embroidery hoop

Embroidery thread in medium green, light pink and medium pink

Paper for tracing pattern

Disappearing ink marker

30 × 40mm glass cabochon

30 × 40mm wooden oval base

Decoupage

Brooch back

Jewellery glue

EQUIPMENT

Pencil

Scissors

Embroidery needle

Paintbrush

ADVANCED

wooden scallops necklace

This wooden scallop necklace is such a pretty and modern accessory. The minty colours are great for any time of year, though it would be fun to use other colour schemes, too. I think deep jewel tones would be so perfect for autumn, or you could use metallic colours for a fabulous winter version. Take the whole necklace to the next level and decoupage pretty papers or fabric over the scallops.

ADVANCED

INSTRUCTIONS

1. Paint the wooden scallops, mixing and matching colours. Play with layout, varying the scallops so you don't have two of the same colour next to each other.

2. Using the gold pen, draw angled lines across the scallops, changing the directions and where the lines meet.

3. When dry, brush the scallops lightly with satin decoupage – the sealant will keep the paint from scratching off. Any type of sealant will work here. A glossy sealant or even a glitter decoupage would look great, too! Just use what you have in your craft supplies.

4. Connect the scallops with jump rings. When you have connected all nine scallops, add a jump ring to the open hole on each end of the chain of scallops.

5. Cut the 35.5cm (14in) chain in half with wire cutters. Add each end of the chain to the jump rings on the end of the scallop chain. Finish your necklace by adding a large jump ring to the left-hand chain. Add the smaller jump ring and a lobster clasp to the right-hand chain.

MATERIALS

9 wooden semicircles with pre-drilled holes – 15 × 30mm

Acrylic craft paint in four colours

Gold paint pen

Satin decoupage

10 × 9mm jump rings

6mm jump ring

35.5cm (14in) length of gold chain

Lobster clasp

EQUIPMENT

Wire cutters

Round nose pliers

Flat nose pliers

Paintbrush

floating beads necklace

Vintage, charity, or antique shops are all great sources for beads, and you can find unique styles often at a fraction of the cost of craft shops. The beads for this piece came from a vintage necklace that was extremely small and not in the best of shape, so I took it apart and used the materials to create this more modern necklace.

ADVANCED

INSTRUCTIONS

1. Cut three lengths of chain, each measuring 46cm (18 in), 51cm (20in) and 56cm (22in). Lay the beads out in a bead tray and measure how far apart you would like them to be on the necklace. In the sample shown, the beads are 3cm (1¼in) apart and the shortest and longest strands have a bead at the centre of the chain. The middle strand has two beads, each 2cm (¾in) from the centre of the chain.

2. Feed a crimp bead onto the smallest strand and add a decorative bead. Place the decorative bead where you would like it on the chain and crimp the bead just below it. Add another crimp bead to the strand and crimp this in place above the decorative bead. Now the bead will be held in place by two crimp beads.

3. Continue adding beads onto the three strands, with the smaller beads towards the ends of the strands. On the sample necklace there are 13 beads on the smallest strand, 14 on the middle strand and 15 on the longest. You could also place the beads on the strand at random intervals for a more free-form appearance.

4. Clamp the connectors to the end of each chain. Open a 6mm jump ring and add the right side connector loops for the chains to the ring, as well as a lobster clasp. Close the ring. Repeat for the left side of the connector loops and the other 6mm jump ring. Before closing the ring, add a closed 9mm jump ring to the chain as well. This will finish the necklace closure.

MATERIALS

Assortment of beads in graduating sizes

153cm (60in) length of 1mm gold chain

2 × 1.5mm crimp beads per bead used in the necklace

6 × chain connectors

2 × 6mm jump rings

9mm jump ring

Lobster clasp

EQUIPMENT

Needle nose pliers

Flat nose pliers

Crimping pliers

Wire cutters

Bead tray

cluster pendant

This design is such a pretty way to highlight a large teardrop bead. The necklace shown here has a graduated ombré colour scheme, but you could mix and match it with a variety of colours. A black and white or neutral version would look beautiful, too.

INSTRUCTIONS

1. Place the pendant bead on a head pin and form a loop at the top. Add all the small beads to head pins and form loops at the tops of these.

2. Cut a 2.5cm (1in) length of chain. Find the centre of the remaining 61cm (24in) length of chain and add a jump ring to the central link. Add the 2.5cm (1in) chain to the jump ring and close it.

3. Open the loop at the top of the pendant bead and add the loop to the bottom link of the 2.5cm (1in) chain. Keeping the loop open, add two of the 3mm bead loops to the pendant loop as well, then close it.

4. Add the smaller beads to the links on the 2.5cm (1 in) chain with the larger beads closest to the pendant and the smaller beads towards the jump ring. Reserve eight of the beads – four 2.5mm and four 1.5mm beads.

5. Add the remaining beads along the necklace chain, spacing them randomly along the central 30.5cm (12in) of the chain.

6. Finish the necklace by adding two jump rings to each end of the chain and a lobster clasp to one of the jump rings.

MATERIALS

Large pendant – sample is 30 × 40mm (1¼ × 1½in)

4 × 3mm beads

9 × 2.5mm beads

8 × 1.5mm beads

22 × head pins

63.5cm (25in) length of rose gold chain

3 × 3mm jump rings

Lobster clasp

EQUIPMENT

Needle nose pliers

Flat nose pliers

Wire cutters

ADVANCED

bead and chain bracelet

Always save small lengths of chain – don't ever throw them away. They are perfect for pieces like this fun bracelet.

INSTRUCTIONS

1. Separate the four 14cm (5½in) length chain strands and place them in two groups of two. Add the ends of two of the chains to one of the 4mm rings and loop the ring through the right loop on one of the end connectors. Close the ring.

2. Repeat for the second set of two chains, adding the rings to the left loops on the other side of the end connector.

3. Add a rhinestone connector to each end of the rhinestone strand. Place a 4mm jump ring through the loop at one end of the strand and add this ring to the middle loop of the end connector.

4. Feed the chains and rhinestone strand through the loop bead.

5. Add jump rings to the other ends of the chains and rhinestone strand, matching up the way the chains are attached to the first end connector. Connect these rings to the opposite loops on the other end connector.

6. Add a 6mm jump ring to the right-hand end connector and add a lobster clasp to the ring.

7. Add the three rhinestone beads to head pins and form loops at the tops of the beads. Add these loops to one end of the 6.5cm (2½in) strand of chain. Add the other end of the chain to the opposite end connector with a 6mm jump ring.

MATERIALS

2 × end connectors with 3 rings on each side of loop

2 × 6mm jump rings

6 × 4mm jump rings

6.5cm (2½in) length of chain

4 × different types of small chain – 14cm (5½in) length

14cm (5½in) length of 3mm rhinestone strand trim

2 × rhinestone connectors

3 × head pins

3 × assorted colour and size rhinestone beads

Decorative loop bead with large opening

Lobster clasp

EQUIPMENT

Wire cutters

Round nose pliers

Flat nose pliers

ADVANCED

TIP

Look for beads with large openings near the leather bracelet section of your local craft shop. They are designed to fit over larger leather strips, but they work perfectly for holding multiple chains, such as those used in this bracelet.

crystallised hoop earrings

All you need are tiny little seed beads to take a set of gold hoop earrings from plain to fabulous. This project is also a great way to give old earrings new life. If you have some gold earrings that are a little tarnished, just cover them up with rows and rows of pretty little beads.

ADVANCED

MATERIALS

2 × 35mm (1¼in) gold hoop earrings

24-gauge gold wrapping wire

Seed beads

EQUIPMENT

Wire cutters

Flat nose pliers

Round nose pliers

INSTRUCTIONS

1. Open up the hoop earring to make wrapping as easy as possible. Cut a length of wire approximately 38cm (15in) long. Place the wire along the side edge of the hoop earring and hold it in place with your left hand. Using either your hand or the pliers, wrap the wire tightly around the hoop three times. Make sure to cover the sharp end of the wire as you wrap.

2. Thread approximately 5cm (2in) of seed beads to the wire, pressing the beads up on the wire to the point where you stopped wrapping. Hold the beads tightly to the end and wrap the wire with the beads around the hoop. Keep the beads and wire as tight as possible around the hoop. Make sure there aren't any spaces between the beads. Wrap until you've almost reached the uncovered wire.

3. Add more beads and continue wrapping until you have covered as much of the hoop as desired. When you have finished wrapping the bead-covered wire, wrap the wire without beads around the hoop tightly three times. Cut the wire and press the cut end tightly to the hoop with flat nose pliers.

4. Repeat for the second earring, making sure the bead section covers the same amount of the hoop as the first earring.

bars and beads necklace

It is so easy to create your own unique chains by simply connecting brass bars with small beads. Keep them simple and layer multiples together, or add a pretty pendant or charm to the chain for even more fun! This necklace is perfect for wearing with other shorter pieces as well – it would look so pretty paired with a small, embroidered necklace or the dipped crystal pendant on page 20 .

page 20

INSTRUCTIONS

1. Begin by adding all the beads to eye pins. Create a loop at the other end of all of the pins.

2. Form the smaller chain by adding an eye pin loop to the bottom hole of a brass connector. Add the other eye loop on the bead to another brass connector. Continue connecting brass connectors to the bead loops, interspersing four of the 8mm beads in between the 6mm beads randomly.

3. Continue creating the chain in this way until it measures 53.5cm (21in). End the chain with a connector bar.

4. Set the smaller chain aside and create another chain with the remaining bars and beads. Place the 8mm beads randomly throughout this chain as well. The finished chain should measure 61cm (24in).

5. Connect the two chains so the smaller chain rests in the centre with a 9mm jump ring on each side. Add another jump ring to the ring on the right-hand side and add a lobster clasp to this ring. Close the ring to finish the closure.

MATERIALS

39 × 18mm brass connector bars

9 × 8mm beads

28 × 6mm beads

37 × eye pins

3 × 9mm jump rings

Lobster clasp

EQUIPMENT

Round nose pliers

Flat nose pliers

Wire cutters

ADVANCED

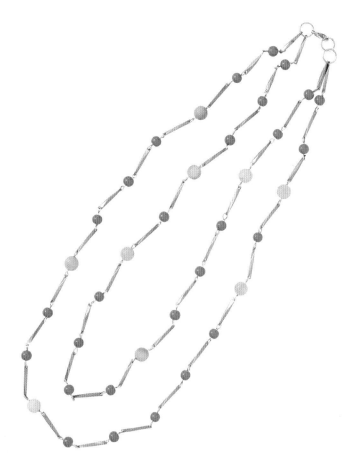

felt hedgehog brooch

This charming brooch is perfect for adding a little style and fun to an outfit. Cute hedgehogs bearing heart-shaped flowers are always in style! See pages 122–124 for help with embroidery techniques.

INSTRUCTIONS

1. Using a pencil, trace the hedgehog template (see page 125) onto a separate piece of paper.

2. Iron fusible webbing to the back of your fabric piece. Trace in pencil, then cut out the shape of the hedgehog's spiky body – you don't need to cut out the head or feet. Remove the paper backing from the webbing.

3. Fuse the fabric to the ivory wool felt by ironing lightly. Place an ironing cloth or a scrap of fabric over the wool felt to protect it.

4. Using the disappearing ink marker, trace the nose and feet of the hedgehog onto the felt, then trace the little heart flower as well.

5. Place the felt in the embroidery hoop. Using a backstitch, embroider the nose, feet and just inside the fabric edge of the hedgehog with three strands of grey embroidery thread. Make a French knot for the eye. Embroider the flower with three strands of green embroidery thread and backstitch the stem.

Use three strands of dark pink thread and a satin stitch to embroider the heart.

6. Remove the felt from the hoop. Draw a 5cm (2in) circle around the hedgehog design and cut out.

7. Cut out a 7.5cm (3in) circle from the raspberry wool felt using pinking shears. Layer together the pink circle, the circle of heavyweight interfacing and then the hedgehog design. Using three strands of the turquoise thread, attach the ivory felt circle to the raspberry felt with a blanket stitch.

8. Sew the brooch back to the reverse side of the raspberry felt using the dark pink thread.

MATERIALS

12.5cm (5in) square of wool felt in ivory

7.5cm (3in) square of wool felt in raspberry pink

4cm (1½in) square of fabric

Embroidery thread in grey, dark pink, green and turquoise

4.5cm (1¾in) circle of heavyweight interfacing

Fusible webbing

Brooch back

Disappearing ink marker

Paper for tracing pattern

EQUIPMENT

Pencil

Scissors

Iron

Embroidery needle

Pinking shears

7.5cm (3in) embroidery hoop

necktie cuff

I love repurposing things – creating something new from something old is so much fun. This sweet bracelet is made from a man's tie, so the cost to create it is minimal and you have all the fun of that menswear look, but dressed up with a feminine flower piece.

INSTRUCTIONS

1. Cut two sections of the tie, each 18cm (7in) long, taking one piece from the 6cm (2¼in) wide section and the other from a narrower part of the tie. Lay the narrow piece over the wider piece so that both ends line up and measure 6cm (2¼in) from top to bottom. Sew through each of the ends to hold the pieces in place.

2. On the right-hand end of the fabric, lay the strip of leather face down and line the edges up. Sew the leather and tie together with a 6mm (¼in) seam allowance.

3. Fold the leather to the right side, then fold in half. Turn the tie to the reverse side, fold the leather under 6mm (¼in) and lay it over the end of the tie. Sew in place. This will create the leather tab at the end of the bracelet.

4. Repeat for the other end of the tie. Add the snap fasteners to the tabs following the manufacturer's instructions.

5. Cut another thin section of the tie approximately 2.5 × 7.5cm (1 × 3in). Wrap around the centre of the cuff and overlap on the back. Fold the end under and hand stitch it into place.

6. Position the enamel flower at the centre front of the cuff and hand stitch securely in place.

MATERIALS

Necktie

Enamel flower bead

2 × strips of narrow leather –
5 × 7.5cm (2 × 2½in)

2 × heavy duty, decorative snap fasteners

Thread to match leather and necktie

Tissue paper

EQUIPMENT

Scissors

Sewing machine

Hammer

Needle

TIP

Sewing with leather can sometimes be tricky, but follow these tips to make it easier: always switch your sewing machine needle out for a heavy duty needle, and if you find the machine is refusing to feed the leather through, lay a piece of tissue paper above and below the leather. Sew through the tissue and tear it away once you have finished.

ADVANCED

embroidered fox necklace

Our dapper little fox is sure to add some fun and style to any outfit. He is created with basic embroidery stitches, so even if you have never tried embroidery before, this is a great piece to begin with. If you have more time, you could even fill in the embroidery with satin stitches for an all-over design. See pages 122–124 for help with embroidery techniques.

See pages 122–124

INSTRUCTIONS

1. Trace the fox pattern (see page 125) onto the fabric with the disappearing ink marker. Place the fabric in the embroidery hoop.

2. Stitch the fox outline using a backstitch and changing colours as necessary. Embroider French knots for the eyes and nose (see page 123). It is important to keep the back of the embroidery as smooth as possible, because the piece will be mounted on wood and any knots will cause bumps in the fabric.

3. Follow the instructions on the hoop necklace frame for mounting. If the top fabric is thin, consider adding a lining fabric or a small piece of felt to give the piece cushioning and stability.

4. Add the 10mm jump ring to the section at the top of the hoop so the jump ring sits around the top screw.

5. Feed the chain through the jump ring and finish with the 6mm jump ring and a lobster clasp.

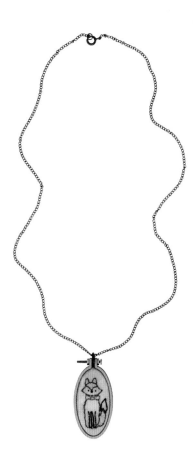

ADVANCED

MATERIALS
12.5cm (5in) square of fabric

Disappearing ink marker

Embroidery thread in black, rust and green

10mm jump ring

6mm jump ring

Lobster clasp

71cm (28in) length of small chain

Jewellery glue

EQUIPMENT
3.4 × 6.2mm (1¼ × 2¼in) embroidery hoop necklace frame

7.5cm (3in) embroidery hoop

Needle

Scissors

Wire cutters

Round nose pliers

Flat nose pliers

TIP
Once you've started embroidering jewellery, you won't want to stop! There are so many pretty options for designs as well – you can find inspiration in vintage styles, modern aztec shapes and even by stitching around the designs in fabric.

beaded drop earrings

Faceted crystals were used to make these gorgeous drop earrings – the perfect accessory to take any outfit up a notch or two. The crystals will catch the light and shimmer every time you move. They will look like you found them at a high-end boutique even though it costs a fraction of the boutique pricing to create them.

INSTRUCTIONS

1. To make the first earring, place a 15mm bead onto a head pin, then add a spacer bead and one of the 6mm crystals. Create a loop at the top of the crystal bead.

2. Add seven of the beads to head pins and create loops at the top of each of the beads.

3. Cut a 15mm (⅝in) length of chain. Add the top loop of the large bead stack to the bottom link of the chain and while the loop is open, add two loops of the little beads, then close the stacked bead loop.

4. Continue adding small bead loops up along the length of chain. You should have five beads on the chain.

5. Add the top loop of chain to the loop at the bottom of the ear wire.

6. Repeat for the second earring.

MATERIALS

2 × 15mm crystal beads

2 × crystal bead spacers

16 × 6mm crystal beads

16 × silver head pins

2.5cm (1in) length of silver chain

2 × silver ear wires

EQUIPMENT

Wire cutters

Round nose pliers

Flat nose pliers

TIP

You can easily adjust the length of this style of earring by adding or removing links of the chain. If you want a dressier version, cut a longer chain and add more crystals along the length. You can also adjust the size, adding larger crystals towards the bottom and smaller crystals at the top of the chain. A very simple version would be to remove the chain entirely and just connect the stacked beads directly onto the ear wire. Any option would look pretty!

ADVANCED

braided chain necklace

This colourful necklace is a great statement piece and such a cute way to add style to a simple outfit.

INSTRUCTIONS

1. Cut three 123cm (48in) lengths from each of the three shades of embroidery thread – so nine in total. Knot the nine strands together 5cm (2in) from the end. Separate the thread so you have three strands of each colour and braid them together – not too tightly – until you have a 38cm (15in) length of braid. You can pin the tip of the braid to keep it steady as you wrap.

2. Cut five 183cm (72in) lengths of thread, creating a mixture between the three colours. Thread these five strands onto the embroidery needle. Thread the strands through the knot at the top of the braid and pull the threads through until the ends match the length of the loose ends of the braid above the knot.

3. Lay the large flat chain on a surface, and lay the braid along the bottom edge so the knot is aligned with the first link of chain. Using the loose thread on the needle, sew the braid to the chain by looping through the chain and run the needle through the braid, then back around the chain. Depending on the size of chain, you will need one or two loops per chain.

4. When you have worked approximately three links of chain, lay the rhinestone strand along the side of the chain, between the braid and the chain. Continue working

the braid and chain together, but pass the thread between the rhinestones on the strand as you go. When you get to the end of the rhinestone strand you should have about three links of chain left. Sew the braid to these links, then knot the braid at the last chain. Unravel the braid and trim the ends of the threads to match the other side.

5. Cut the gold chain into two 28cm (11in) lengths. Fold each chain in half. Add the two ends of one chain to the top link of the large chain on one side, and repeat for the other side. Add a jump ring at the top centre of each of the gold chain pieces. Finish by adding a lobster clasp to one side.

MATERIALS

3 × colours of crewel embroidery thread

22.5cm (10in) length of 7mm rhinestone strand

33cm (13in) length of large flat chain

56cm (22in) length of medium weight gold chain

2 × 9mm jump rings

Lobster clasp

EQUIPMENT

Wire cutters

Round nose pliers

Embroidery needle with large eye

TIP

If you find the thread or rhinestones are shifting around, add a small dot of jewellery glue under the loose sections to hold everything in place.

ADVANCED

multi-chain bracelet

You can create such unique pieces of jewellery by mixing up the materials within a project. This bracelet has such a fun style with its combination of colourful chains, rhinestones and a fabric snap closure.

INSTRUCTIONS

1. Cut out the fabric strips. Centre the fusible interfacing on the back side of each strip and iron into place.

2. Fold one of the fabric strips in half, by bringing the two short ends together, with the back side of the fabric facing you. Sew along each side leaving a 12mm (½in) seam allowance. Trim the seams. Turn the tube right side out and press. Repeat for the second fabric strip.

3. Place the open end of the fabric strip around the flat side of a D-ring. Fold the fabric over twice to form a little hem and hold the ring in place. Sew along the folded edge. Repeat for the second strip and D-ring.

4. Place the snaps in the fabric strips, taking care to follow the manufacturer's instructions.

5. If necessary, cut the lengths of chain and rhinestone strands to size. If you are using rhinestones, add connector pieces to each end of the strand (these are little clamps with a ring on one end).

6. Add a jump ring to each end of the chain pieces. Place the jump rings on one end of the chains and D-ring and attach the other ends of the chains to the remaining D-ring. Check that the fabric strips are facing the right way so the snaps meet.

TIP

For an alternative to rhinestones, create a small strand of beads to add in with the chains. This will also add a little more colour and style to the bracelet.

MATERIALS

2 × pieces of fabric – 5 × 15cm (2 × 6in)

2 × pieces of mid-weight fusible interfacing 2.5 13cm (1 × 5in)

2 × D-rings

2 × decorative snap fasteners

10 × 9mm jump rings

10cm (5 × 4in) lengths of assorted chain and/or rhinestones

Thread to match fabric

EQUIPMENT

Sewing machine

Hammer (for snaps)

Scissors

Round nose pliers

Flat nose pliers

Wire cutters

Iron

equipment

Now that you are starting your adventure in jewellery making, you will need to gather up a few tools and supplies to make your projects. These are just the basics in the way of tools, but you will find that you can create a huge variety of projects with them. You can make jewellery with more than just the traditional jewellery tools, which are sold separately at most craft stores, online jewellery supply shops, or in kits. Sewing, embroidery and even just general crafting supplies can be used to create accessory pieces that are perfect for your style and so much more fun than shop-bought pieces.

jewellery tools

Round nose pliers: These pliers have round tips that taper to a small end. They are perfect for wire wrapping, creating eye loops and holding pieces while you're working with them.

Flat nose pliers: These pliers are best friends with your round nose pliers. You will often use them together. They are perfect for opening and closing jump rings, flattening wire that you've wrapped and holding pieces while you work.

Wire cutters: I recommend having a few different levels of wire cutters. Jewellery wire cutters are perfect for cutting chains, thin wires and even some styles of cording. You can use thinner wire shears for delicate wires and small metal chains. Heavy duty wire cutters (or even bolt cutters) from the hardware store come in handy for cutting heavy-duty chain links.

Crimping pliers: These handy pliers are just what you need to clamp those tiny crimping beads around your wire and beading cord. Their dual crimping sections make it easy to crimp the beads tightly, so you don't have to worry about your beads falling off your gorgeous necklace while you're wearing it.

Rulers: A 30cm (12in) ruler is ideal, as is a fabric measuring tape. Make sure that they show both imperial and metric measurements.

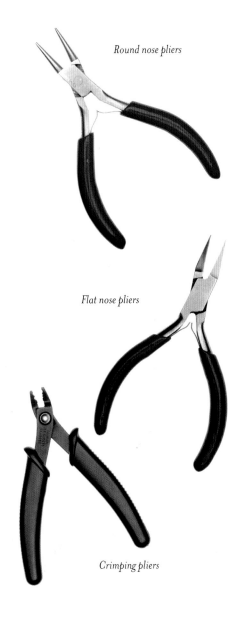

Round nose pliers

Flat nose pliers

Crimping pliers

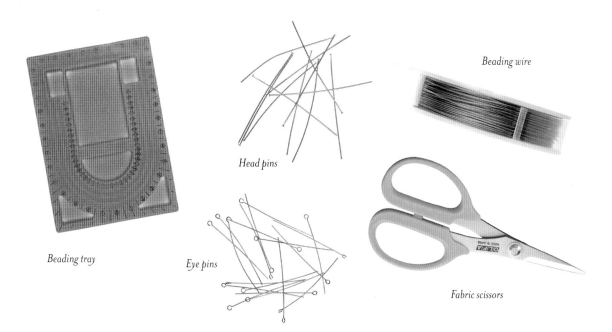

Beading tray

Head pins

Beading wire

Eye pins

Fabric scissors

OPTIONAL BUT RECOMMENDED:

Beading tray: This tray is designed to provide you with a place to lay out your pieces, check the measurements and keep your beads from rolling off your work surface.

Ring mandrel: You can create rings with anything round; a marker or paintbrush handle will be fine. But if you're going to be making rings on a regular basis, I highly recommend a ring mandrel. These handy tools are marked with ring sizes, so if you're making rings for more than just yourself you can easily see what size to make them.

jewellery supplies

Head pins: These incredibly useful pins are wires of different lengths or thicknesses that have a small metal cap at one end. They are ideal for holding beads that you want to attach to a chain or to other beads. You can find head and eye pins in most craft shops and online jewellery shops in different metals and styles. You can also find decorative head pins: these are head pins, but instead of a plain metal cap on one end there is a small decorative cap. They are a fun way to add a little extra pizzazz to a piece. Choose head and eye pins that are the right length and thickness for the beads you are using.

Eye pins: Like head pins, these wires come in a variety of lengths and thicknesses. These pins have a loop already created on one end.

Beading wire or cording: Beading wire comes in a variety of materials and weights. Each of the projects in this book that use it specify a certain weight of wire. For future projects,

you'll want to choose a wire that is flexible and appropriate to the project and bead size. The wire should easily pass through the opening in the beads you are using.

Jewellery findings: These are all the components needed to construct your jewellery designs. They are usually made of metal, and include items such as ear wires for creating hook or dangle earrings, jump rings that twist open to connect pieces to stringing material and lobster clasps to fasten necklaces and bracelets together.

sewing supplies

Sewing machine: Some of the projects in this book take a little sewing. The stitching is mostly simple and is perfect for beginners. You can add so much variety to a jewellery piece when you start adding in fabrics.

A basic sewing machine is all you need – something that will make a simple straight stitch is fine. You'll want to have needles that are appropriate for the fabric or material you are using as well. You can find all-purpose, leather, knit, or other needles at your local fabric shop.

Fabric scissors: These are not to be confused with paper scissors. Pick up a pair of fabric scissors at your fabric shop and keep them exclusively for cutting fabric. You'll find that they stay sharp much longer and you will have a much easier time cutting your fabric with them.

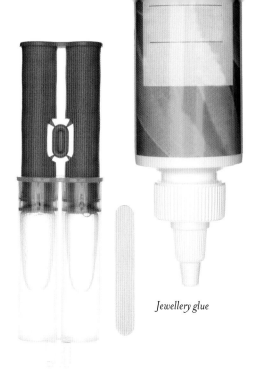

Jewellery glue

Hand sewing needles

Hand sewing needles: I like to use hand sewing needles that are nice and sharp and have a large eye. You can purchase these at your local craft shop in multi-size packages with a few different options on size. If you are sewing beads to a project, check that your needle will fit through the bead easily before beginning. If you need them, beading needles can be found in the jewellery section of craft shops. These are usually thinner and have very narrow eyes so they can pass easily through most beads.

Thread: All the thread used in these projects is multi-purpose. Choose thread that closely matches your fabrics or beads so it blends in with your projects.

Iron and ironing board: While these aren't technically sewing supplies, they are helpful when working with fabrics. Ironing your project between steps and after finishing will give your pieces a more professional look, keep your projects neat and make your seams and measurements more accurate.

general crafting supplies

Paper scissors: Perfect for cutting out patterns or paper jewellery crafting supplies. These won't be as sharp as fabric scissors and can be found in any shop that carries basic office or craft supplies.

Paintbrushes: You can use traditional inexpensive paint or foam brushes for the projects in this book. Choose your brush size based on the dimensions of the project you are working on. A thin paintbrush is great for applying decoupage, and a larger foam brush would be great for painting a bangle.

Decoupage: I use decoupage often in my jewellery work – either for applying paper to a base piece, or for adhering fabric embroidery pieces to glass cabochons. The decoupage makes a nice clear glue and is easy to apply. It comes in a variety of finishes; glossy, matt, fabric, paper and even glitter. I mostly use matt finish, but on pieces such as the map bangle on page 39, I like a glossy or satin finish to add a little sheen.

Jewellery glue: I prefer E-6000 as my jewellery glue, but I know that it has a strong odour that bothers some people. You can use any jewellery glue that you prefer, just remember to use all of them in a well-ventilated area. Choose a glue that is very strong and sets quickly. I recommend trying a sample piece if you haven't worked with a glue brand before; that way if it isn't perfect, you haven't ruined your finished piece.

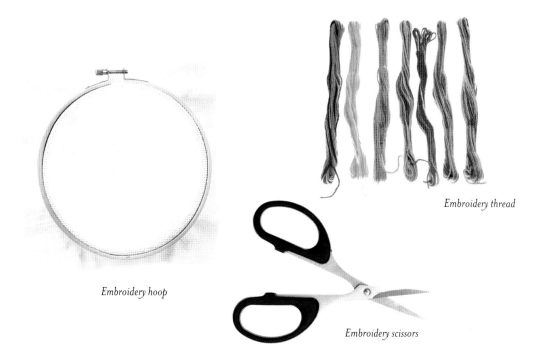

Embroidery hoop

Embroidery thread

Embroidery scissors

Spray finish: These are aerosol finishes that you apply as you would spray paint. They come in different finishes, such as glossy, matt and satin.

Stabiliser: Stabilisers are interfacings that come in a variety of weights. Heavyweight stabilisers give strength to larger pieces, and thinner stabilisers make your fabric stronger and easier to sew with.

Greaseproof paper: This useful paper is found in most supermarkets. It is matt on one side and glossy on the other, and is perfect for stabilising fabric in order to print on it. You can also use it for stencils by simply ironing the shiny side straight onto your fabric before peeling it off.

embroidery supplies

Small embroidery hoop: These can be found at almost any craft shop. Small hoops work well for the pieces in this book because you don't need to waste a lot of fabric to fit in a larger hoop. I use a 7.5cm (3in) wooden hoop for most jewellery projects.

Embroidery needle: Embroidery needles have larger eyes, but are just as sharp as sewing needles (unlike yarn needles). The larger eyes are necessary because you will be working with thicker threads.

Embroidery thread: I use two different types of thread: standard embroidery thread and pearl cotton. Embroidery thread is made up of six very small strands. I usually separate the strands when I'm using embroidery thread, two or three strands often work very well for small embroidery pieces. Pearl cotton is not separated – you stitch with the complete thread. It has a slight texture to it and works very well for backstitching, and flowers or lettering, where you want a little texture to your stitches.

Embroidery scissors: These are not required, but I recommend them for your embroidery pieces. They are small, so they are easy to keep with your work, and they are usually very sharp – perfect for snipping small threads and keeping your embroidery work neat.

Disappearing ink marker: These markers can be found at your local fabric shop or online. I prefer these for transferring all my embroidery work, as well as marking locations when sewing. They are great for noting where snap fasteners and sewing lines should be. With these markers, the ink disappears over time or you can remove it with a damp cloth. I recommend removing the marker lines before putting your embroidery in its final setting.

jewellery techniques

Here you will find some basic jewellery-making techniques that are used throughout the book. We are going to be working with all sorts of fun tools on these projects, and with tools come all sorts of opportunities to get hurt if you aren't careful. All of the tools I recommend are completely safe, as long as you follow some basic safety precautions.

safety precautions

Wire cutters: When you are cutting wires, pins, or chains, there is a good chance that the end you are cutting will fly off. We want to avoid this, as well as any trips to the eye doctor. When using wire cutters or any type of snips, point the flat end of the cutters away from your face. It also helps to place your other hand behind the wire cutters to catch the piece you are cutting off. This will keep your work area neat and will prevent you from leaving little shards of pins and wire all over the floor.

Scissors: I recommend using very sharp scissors for embroidery and fabric cutting; they will make your projects go much more smoothly. Use caution when cutting so that you avoid snipping fingers, or anything else, accidentally.

Glue guns and glue: Glue guns get very hot. To avoid burning yourself or your work surface, place a heat resistant mat under your glue gun. This will catch any drips and protect your table. Avoid touching the sides of the glue gun when it is hot, and definitely don't touch the glue itself. Hot glue can cause very painful burns and blisters. You will want to protect your work surface from jewellery glue as well, and use it in a well-ventilated area.

With all pliers and other tools, use caution. Please watch children around all your supplies as well.

how to open a jump ring

Jump rings are metal rings with a cut in them. They come in a wide variety of sizes, colours and thicknesses. Choose the ring size and colour that works best for your project. To open jump rings, hold the ring with flat nose pliers on one side. Hold the opposite side with round nose pliers. Always open jump rings by twisting the open ends away from each other, so the ends stay in a vertical line. Don't open them by pulling the ring wider, or horizontally. This distorts and weakens the shape. Close the ring by twisting the ends back together. Make sure the metal pieces are touching and closed tightly, otherwise wire or cording could slip through the hole.

adding a bead to a head pin and forming a loop at the top

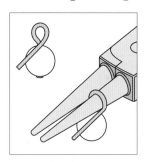

Place your bead on a head pin. Make sure the head pin you choose is long enough to extend over the top of the bead to form the loop size you want to create.

Place the wire in the round nose pliers, so that the bead is just below the section where the pliers meet. The end of the wire should be pointing upwards. The tips of the pliers are angled, so keep in mind where you place the wire in the pliers. If the bead is further back towards the handle, you will have a larger loop.

A smaller loop can be created towards the tips of the pliers. To start the loop, bend the pin at a slight angle at the top of the bead.

Wrap the pin wire around one side of your round nose pliers, away from the way you created the bend, to make a loop. Wrap the wire tightly around the nose of the pliers, and cross the end of the wire over the bead so the wire makes an 'X'.

Clip off the end of the wire without the bead, just above the bead, using your wire cutters. Make sure to point the flat side of the cutters away from you.

Bend your pin wire just a little more to create a complete loop. Make sure that when you open the loop that you twist the wire open, rather than separate it, just like a jump ring.

using cording and crimp beads

You can use plastic, metal or thread cording to string beads.

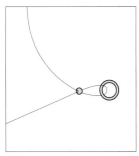

Usually we finish a bead strand with a jump ring; this makes it easy to add to other strands or necklace closures.

I recommend cutting your cording at least 10cm (4in) longer than the length you'll need your strand to be. That will allow you plenty of cording for looping around the jump ring.

To begin, thread a crimp bead onto your length of cording and loop the end around a jump ring, then thread the cord back through the crimp bead.

Place the crimp pliers around the crimp bead. Use the second opening from the tip of the pliers. Without tightening the pliers, move the bead up close to the jump ring, but not touching it. Crimp the bead flat.

Place the crimped bead in the opening closest to the tip of the crimping pliers. Angle the crimped bead vertically in the opening. Crimp the bead a second time, so the bead is folded in half.

As you thread the beads, make sure they cover the small end of the cording as well. Finish your strand as desired.

finishing a necklace

One of the most common ways to finish off a necklace is with a lobster closure. Now that you know how to use a jump ring, these are really easy.

Add the lobster end of the closure to one of your chains with a small jump ring, and add a large jump ring to the other end of the chain. You can also use a toggle closure. This is a large ring for one side of the necklace, and a post for the other side.

Attach each piece to the sides of your necklace chain with jump rings.

finishing a stretch bracelet

SURGEON'S KNOT

Begin the knot by passing the left end over the right, then wrapping it around the right side, in the same way that you would start any knot or tie your shoe.

To finish the knot, repeat the process in the opposite direction, but instead of wrapping the right piece of cording around the left just once, wrap it twice, then pull the knot tight. This gives the knot a little extra stability.

OVERHAND KNOT

Make a loop in the cording or material about 2.5cm (1in) from one end. Pass the short end of the cording through the loop and adjust the knot so it's about 1.25cm (½in) from the end of the cording. Pull the knot tight. You can create these anywhere along cording or threads for a very tight knot, and they work especially well for finishing ends of cording, holding beads in place, or keeping threads from unravelling.

LARK'S HEAD KNOT

The Lark's Head knot is the knot most frequently used for tying cording to rings, handles, or other hardware. Fold the cording in half and run the folded point of the cording around the ring or handle, from top to bottom (away from you). Open up the little loop made at the top of the cording after it's gone through the ring. Pass the two ends of the cording through the cording loop and pull tight.

embroidery techniques

Even if you haven't ever done a stitch of embroidery, you can easily complete all the projects in this book – and start a new hobby that will have you wanting to embroider more and more. All the projects use the basic stitches you will find here. Feel free to experiment – if a piece is just outlined, you can add in some satin stitching or change up the design with little flowers or other pretty details. Get adventurous!

tracing your pattern

You can use all sorts of different methods and materials to transfer your design onto your fabric. I prefer a simple method, using a window and a disappearing ink marker. Print out your design onto standard copy paper. Tape your design up on a window during the day so the light comes through the paper. Tape your fabric piece over the design and the light from the window will work as a lightbox to shine the design through the fabric. Trace your design with a disappearing ink marker. Remove the materials from the window and you are ready to get started.

placing fabric in a hoop

The first step in stitching a fabulous piece of embroidery is to place your fabric in a hoop. An embroidery hoop keeps your fabric stable and makes stitching much easier – if you don't use a hoop your fabric is more likely to have little puckers around the stitching.

Cut your fabric at least 5cm (2in) bigger than the diameter of your embroidery hoop. Separate the hoop into the two pieces; you might have to loosen the screw at the top of the hoop. Place the smaller ring of the hoop on a flat surface, then lay your fabric over the hoop, making sure that the entire ring is covered. Lay the top piece of the hoop over the fabric and press down, so the fabric is caught between the two hoops. Tighten the screw at the top of the hoop to hold the fabric firmly in place. Pull on the edges of the fabric to pull it tight in the hoop – you want the fabric taut but not stretched in the hoop. Tighten the screw a little more if you need to.

knotting your thread

When you are hand sewing, you usually form a little knot at the end of your thread to keep the thread from pulling all the way through the fabric. Sometimes in embroidery that is okay, for example, if you are creating some hoop art or something that isn't framed. But in jewellery embroidery, we really don't want knots behind our work causing little bumps in the fabric. These will show up especially if you are wrapping your fabric around a cabochon.

To keep your thread from pulling through, when you make your first stitch, pull your thread through and leave an end of about 12mm (½in) on the back side. Hold this end in place with your finger. Make your next stitch, but as you put your needle from back to front again, move the end of the thread so that the stitch on the back of the piece covers the loose end. Keep stitching, continuing to cover the end of the thread as you go. You might need to move the thread a bit so it is caught by the stitches. Continue until you have the thread end completely covered on the back side. This will hold the end of the thread in place without a knot on the back side.

basic stitches
RUNNING STITCH

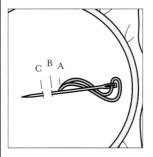

This simple stitch is perfect for outlining pieces, sewing pieces of a project together and adding a decorative look.

Bring your needle up at A. Bring it back down at B and back up at C. You can pull your thread through after each stitch, or you can do several stitches on one pass with the needle and then pull your needle through afterwards.

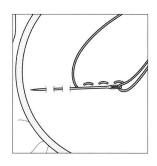

Keep this pattern throughout the stitch, with the length of the stitches, and distances between the stitches, remaining the same throughout the piece.

BACKSTITCH

A backstitch is often used for outlining designs and lettering.

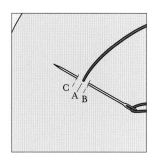

Bring your needle up about 4mm (⅛in) from the beginning of your line. That will be your A point. Pull your thread through. Put your needle back down at B, bring it back up at C.

For the next stitch, you'll repeat the process – up at A, down at B, up at C.

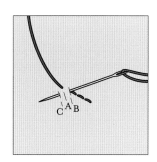

When you get to a point, just make your C point across it. This will allow you to have nice, pointed lines.

STEM STITCH

These are most often used for... wait for it... stems! Great for floral designs and can also be used for outlining and lettering.

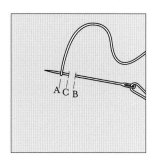

For the stem stitch, the point where your thread comes up is A. Insert your needle at B and bring it back out at C. The distance between A, B and C should be equal.

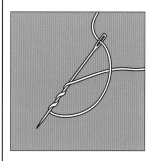

Keep your loose thread above the stitch, and repeat the stitching pattern. Your needle will come out at a point touching the end of the previous stitch.

Continue stitching in this way, following all lines and curves. If your stitches start to 'fall' or don't lay flat on a curve, make a small stitch around the stem stitch to hold it in place.

FRENCH KNOT

These little knots are incredibly versatile! Fast to stitch, they can be used for everything, from eyes to tiny flowers. They are great for adding details to a piece, but you can also create an entire design out of French knots. There are so many options.

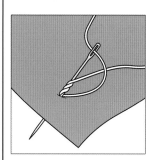

Bring your needle up through the fabric from back to front. Close to the point that the thread comes out of the fabric, hold your needle and wrap the thread around the needle three times. You can wrap your thread around the needle more or fewer times, depending on how big or small of a knot you want.

Hold the tail of the thread in place with your thumb, and with your other hand put the needle point back through the fabric, right next to where you brought it up. Holding the thread as you bring the needle back through, until the very last minute, will keep the knot from tightening too soon or from being too loose of a knot.

Pull the needle through the wrapped thread, holding lightly to the end until it's all pulled through. This will form a French knot.

LAZY DAISY STITCH

These sweet little stitches are just what you need for leaves and simple flower petals.

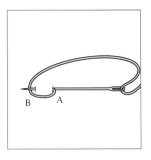

Decide where you want the first petal to be positioned. Insert your needle at the bottom of the petal from the front to the back of the fabric – that will be point A. Bring your needle from the back of the fabric to the front at the top of the petal, but don't pull it all the way through. That's point B. Wrap the thread around the tip of the needle from left to right.

Pull the needle through, keeping it above the wrapped thread. Don't pull too tight or you'll have a line instead of a petal.

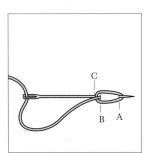

Keeping the petal loose, insert your needle on the outside of the petal at the top – see point C in the diagram below. Bring the needle back up again at point A.

Pull the needle through. This will make a tiny stitch at the top of the petal and hold it in place.

Continue making petals with the bottom points touching to make a flower.

BLANKET STITCH

This is most often used for edging detail, and for sewing one piece of fabric to another. It makes a lovely finishing stitch.

Start by bringing your needle up about 6mm (¼in) below the edge of the top piece of fabric.

Sew a little stitch about ¼in (6mm) from the left of this one, putting the needle 6mm (¼in) below the edge of the felt and bringing it out just above the felt and over the loop of thread.

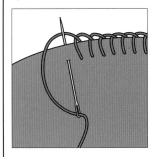

Repeat this last step again to start forming the blanket stitch. Sew all the way around the piece until you come back to the beginning. For the last stitch, loop it through the first stitch to make the thread lay flat.

BULLION STITCH

These are so pretty for flowers – use multiple stitches in a circular pattern for roses, or layer vertical stitches for hyacinths.

Bring the thread up through the fabric at A. Sew a stitch from B back to A, but don't pull the needle all the way through.

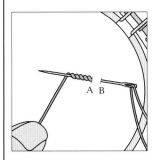

Wrap the loose thread around the needle five or six times. Push the wraps down towards the base of the needle, where it exits the fabric. Wrap more or fewer times, depending on the stitch length you want.

Holding the wraps in place with your thumb, gently pull the needle through so the thread is completely pulled through the wrapped section and the wraps are right up against the fabric. You may need to use your nail to hold the wraps in place as you pull.

To finish, put your needle back through the fabric at the point where you started the stitch. To cause a curve or bow in the stitch, add more wraps than the length of the little stitch you make at the very beginning.

To create a rose, form several small bullion stitches in a curved pattern around a specific point, increasing the length of your stitches (and changing the thread colour if you wish) as you move out from the centre.

patterns

These drawings are to scale. Trace them onto paper and then onto fabric, or cut out as required.

leather chevron necklace *page 64*
Cut three of the larger chevron piece from leather.
Cut three of the smaller chevron piece from fabrics.

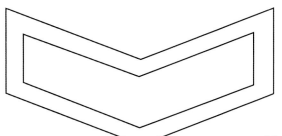

embroidered rose brooch
page 93

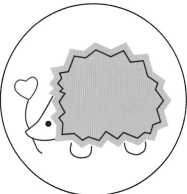

**feather and chain
earrings** *page 50*
Cut two from leather.
Cut one laid this way, then
flip the pattern and cut one
feather reversed.

felt hedgehog brooch *page 104*
Cut the green shape out of fabric. Stitch all
other lines according to the instructions.

daisy earrings *page 47*
Use this pattern for the
left earring, reverse the
pattern for the right
earring. Daisy petals are
stitched with white thread.

cat's meow necklace: face
page 72

cat's meow necklace: ears
page 72
Cut one of the larger shapes
from leather. Cut one of the
smaller shapes from fabric.

embroidered fox necklace
page 108

index

acknowledgements

I would love to thank everyone who made this book possible. Doug, Becka, and Jake – your support means more to me than you know and I'm pretty much the luckiest wife and mom ever. Cin, thank you so much for being the best sister ever, my cheerleader, and my sounding board. Mom and Dad – thank you for encouraging us to be creative and for making art and sewing such an integral part of our growing up. Thank you to my friends and family for your amazing support. A very special thank you to Caroline, Mark, Ellie, Emma, Michael, and the teams at Quintet and Barron's for all your support and for making my dream of writing a book come true.

Quintet would like to thank Hannah-May Chapman for testing the projects.

resources

You can find most of the supplies for the projects in this book at your local craft shop – they are usually well stocked with chains, jump rings, pins, and pretty stones and beads. If I'm not browsing in the craft shops, my favourite place to look for unique findings and beads is *Etsy.com*. There are so many fabulous shops online where you can find beautiful materials to create your projects. Here is a list of some of my favourites:

Most supplies including some fabric, chains and other findings were purchased from Hobbycraft, Beads Direct and Beadworks.

OTHER FABRICS
Blend Fabrics – Good Company, Robert Kaufman – Kona Solids, Michael Miller – Brambleberry Ridge, Rosemilk, Mint by Violet Craft, Various Vintage Fabrics.

ETSY RESOURCES
Wooden Necklace and Brooch Blanks: *www.etsy.com/shop/artbase*
Wooden Bangle Blanks: *www.etsy.com/shop/RocknWoodSupply*
Large End Cap Closures: *www.etsy.com/shop/nottoto*
Brass Connector Beads and Brass Diamond Shapes: *www.etsy.com/shop/rawbrassshop*
Wool Felt: *www.etsy.com/shop/Gingermelon*
Brass Prong Setting: *www.etsy.com/shop/cmyk*
Agate Stones: *www.etsy.com/shop/TheBeadBandit*
Quartz Pieces: *www.etsy.com/shop/CaliGirlBeadShop*
Wood Cloud Piece: *www.etsy.com/shop/Beadeux*
Vintage Style Beads, Brass Details, Dyeable Beads and Acrylic Beads: *www.etsy.com/shop/waytobead*
Mini Hoop Frames for Jewellery: *www.etsy.com/shop/dandelyne*
Mini Masterpiece Frames: *www.etsy.com/shop/eWoodStory*

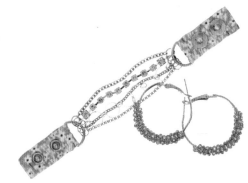